Praise for *Life Lessons and Love Languages*

Gary Chapman's new memoir reminds us how God uses every experience, every turn in life to refine and equip us for usefulness in the kingdom. Be encouraged in your own life by seeing what God has done in Gary's.

MAX LUCADO
Pastor and *New York Times* bestselling author

I can think of few men who have had a greater impact on lives and families than Gary Chapman. Now we have the benefit of an in-depth glimpse into the major influences by which the Lord has shaped Gary into a servant-hearted leader who ministers to others so effectively and faithfully.

JIM DALY
President, Focus on the Family

Like a chat with an old friend, you will love this behind-the-scenes peek at the life and ministry of Dr. Gary Chapman. In *Life Lessons and Love Languages*, Dr. Chapman shares the remarkable journey on which God has led him over the years, eventually becoming one of the best-known figures in Christian ministry. I've known Dr. Chapman for a long time, and he is the real deal—a humble, caring, generous, and wise follower of Christ. This backstory is itself an inspiring lesson about what God can do with someone who says yes to His call.

SHAUNTI FELDHAHN
Social researcher and internationally bestselling author of *For Women Only*, *Surprising Secrets of Highly Happy Marriages*, and *Thriving in Love and Money*

Gary Chapman is like a brother to me, having known him for almost forty years. Yet it's only after reading this book that I feel like I know "the rest of the story," and more about this focused and flexible servant of God. We read in Psalm 71:17, "O God, from my youth you have taught me, and I still proclaim your wondrous deeds" (ESV). The unnamed writer of this psalm, and Gary Chapman, have much in common. Read this short, powerful book to be inspired. I was!

GREG THORNTON
CFO, Moody Bible Institute

Who actually gets to sit down with their favorite author or speaker and really understand who they are? The events that shaped them? This incredible book lets us look "under the hood" at Gary Chapman, to begin to understand how he can be so humble and incredible at changing and impacting literally millions of lives. You and I get to read firsthand the stories, experiences, trials, and amazing life lessons that have shaped Dr. Chapman's life. Even more, reading his insights on all the places God has taken him can take us to a whole new level of trusting and loving Jesus and others. What a powerful, uplifting, inspiring look at someone who defines a life well lived— and challenges us to go do the same for Jesus as well!

JOHN TRENT
Coauthor of *The Blessing*; founder of StrongFamilies.com

Life Lessons *and* Love Languages™

WHAT I'VE LEARNED ON MY UNEXPECTED JOURNEY

Gary Chapman

MOODY PUBLISHERS

CHICAGO

All Scripture quotations, unless otherwise indicated, are taken from the Holy Bible, New International Version®, NIV®. Copyright © 1973, 1978, 1984, 2011 by Biblica, Inc.™ Used by permission of Zondervan. All rights reserved worldwide. www.zondervan.com The "NIV" and "New International Version" are trademarks registered in the United States Patent and Trademark Office by Biblica, Inc.™

Scripture quotations marked (ESV) are from the ESV® Bible (The Holy Bible, English Standard Version®), copyright © 2001 by Crossway, a publishing ministry of Good News Publishers. Used by permission. All rights reserved.

Edited by Elizabeth Cody Newenhuyse
Interior design: Brandi Davis
Cover design: Erik M. Peterson
Cover photograph ©2020 by Brooke Pennington/Grooters Productions

Library of Congress Cataloging-in-Publication Data

Names: Chapman, Gary D., 1938- author.
Title: Life lessons and love languages : what I've learned on my unexpected
    journey / Gary Chapman.
Description: Chicago : Moody Publishers, [2021] | Summary: "Get to know
    Gary Chapman. You just might discover yourself along the way. Many
    people know Gary Chapman as the man who helped the world learn how to
    speak the five love languages. But the thing about Gary is . . . he's
    just a regular guy from Small Town, USA, not all that different from
    you. And in the mirror of Gary's life, you might discover your own
    story, too. In Life Lessons and Love Languages, you'll discern the five
    influences that shape people's lives: home, education, marriage,
    children, and vocation. Even if you don't experience each of these
    influences yourself, you'll benefit from seeing how these pillars of
    human society work together to make productive people. Getting to know
    Gary will be a lot of fun. But getting to know yourself and how your
    world works is a gift that this small-town kid doesn't want you to
    miss"-- Provided by publisher.
Identifiers: LCCN 2020047532 (print) | LCCN 2020047533 (ebook) | ISBN
    9780802423986 (paperback) | ISBN 9780802499790 (ebook)
Subjects: LCSH: Chapman, Gary D., 1938- | Baptists--United
    States--Clergy--Biography. | Christian life--United States. | Conduct of
    life--United States.
Classification: LCC BX6495.C427 A3 2021 (print) | LCC BX6495.C427 (ebook)
    | DDC 286.092 [B]--dc23
LC record available at https://lccn.loc.gov/2020047532
LC ebook record available at https://lccn.loc.gov/2020047533

Originally delivered by fleets of horse-drawn wagons, the affordable paperbacks from D. L. Moody's publishing house resourced the church and served everyday people. Now, after more than 125 years of publishing and ministry, Moody Publishers' mission remains the same—even if our delivery systems have changed a bit. For more information on other books (and resources) created from a biblical perspective, go to www.moodypublishers.com or write to:

Moody Publishers
820 N. LaSalle Boulevard
Chicago, IL 60610

1 3 5 7 9 10 8 6 4 2

Printed in the United States of America

*Dedicated to all those individuals who have cooperated
with God in helping me learn life lessons.*

Contents

Introduction

M any of us are living so fast that we seldom stop to reflect
on what we are doing, why we are doing it, and where it
is leading. We are creatures of action, always doing something,
but seldom taking time to talk to ourselves about the bigger
issues of life. Entertainment, pleasure, and the pursuit of happiness have become the goals of many. Yet even when these goals
are attained, the human spirit cries out for something more.

In the world of technology, humankind has reached heights
never thought imaginable when I was a child. The accessibility
of knowledge on any subject is at our fingertips. We are the
most educated people in history, and yet we still fight each
other like ancient tribal cultures. Why? What do we hope to
accomplish? Where are we going? These are questions faced by
the new generation. We can only hope that they find answers.

However, for those of us who are nearing the end of our
journey, it is also time for reflection. Time to look back and
ask, Where have we been? What have we accomplished? And
what lies ahead? How did I get to where I am? Or how did I
become me?

Having entered the last quarter of my game, I am taking time
to ask that question. I am looking back on a life that has been
extremely satisfying. I have few regrets. I am greatly blessed and

humbled when I take time to meditate on my journey. In the pages ahead, I am sharing my reflections with a desire to encourage those who follow after me.

I believe that too often one generation fails to share with the next the wisdom that has come through the joys and sorrows of life. And sometimes the rising generation has failed to ask questions and listen to older adults. In pursuit of the latest idol, they miss the wisdom right in front of them. It is my desire that my reflections will encourage other "older adults" to do likewise. Published or unpublished, the recording of your journey has the potential of greatly impacting your grandchildren and great-grandchildren. It is also my prayer that younger adults who read these pages will be motivated to reach out to the older adults in their life and ask questions about their life's journey. Their successes you may want to emulate, and their failures you may be able to avoid.

I believe that too often one generation fails to share with the next the wisdom that has come through the joys and sorrows of life. And sometimes the rising generation has failed to ask questions and listen to older adults.

I hope to share with you some of the failures and successes in my own life and what I learned from both. I also want to pay tribute to the many people who have impacted my life. None of us are who we are simply by our own self-efforts. We have been influenced by many people and circumstances.

I could not have planned the life I have lived. Don't get me wrong, I had plans, but most of them did not turn out the way I had imagined. I have become keenly aware of the reality of the ancient Hebrew proverb: "In their hearts humans plan their course, but the LORD establishes their steps" (Prov. 16:9). By the age of seventeen, I did know that I wanted to invest my life in serving Christ by serving people. That plan came to fruition, but never in my wildest dreams would I have imagined what that would look like.

In those early years, if someone had suggested that I would spend half of my life counseling couples, I probably would have asked, "What's a counselor?" The very idea that I would become a writer and author of more than fifty books would have raised the question, "Why would I write a book and what in the world would I say?" Even when I became an author, if someone had predicted that my books would be translated and published in over fifty languages, I likely would have said, "You have got to be kidding!"

If someone had told me that I would earn undergraduate and graduate degrees in anthropology, I would have asked, "What's anthropology?" If someone had told me that I would earn a PhD degree, I likely would have asked, "What does PhD mean?" I could see myself finishing high school and attending college, but after that, I was expecting to "go to work."

I never dreamed that my life would take me to speak at the Pentagon in Washington, DC, or to a gathering of ambassadors to the US from thirty countries, or at a luncheon with Members of Parliament in London, discussing how the church and government could cooperate more fully in meeting human needs. Nor would I have imagined that I would lead marriage and family workshops in more than twenty countries around the world. And I certainly would never have expected to work on the same church staff for fifty years. No, I could not have planned the life I have lived. Yes, I made my plans, but the Lord determined my steps.

In the following pages, I hope to trace the hand of God in using so many people and circumstances to accomplish His plans for my life. I will frame my journey as five major influences on my life. (As you may know, I like the number five.) I will share the lessons I learned along the way, each lesson preparing me for the next step in my journey. I hope that what I share will encourage you in your own journey with God. You too likely have plans for your life, and that is fine; only hold those plans in an open hand to God. He will also direct your steps.

Early Influences from Home

1938–1955

Life in
Small-Town USA

What I share in the next few pages is designed to give you a picture of what life was like growing up in a small North Carolina town with my mom, dad, and sister, Sandra. The first seventeen years of my life, in that setting, greatly influenced my life.

After forty years of doing marriage and family counseling, I am keenly aware that children are strongly impacted by the family in which they grow up. My deepest emotional pain has come from seeing children who grew up with absentee or abusive parents. Much of my life has been spent in trying to help them break the destructive patterns learned in childhood.

Those of us who grew up in stable, loving families are given a distinct advantage in life. For that I am deeply grateful. Sam and Grace, Dad and Mom, were married for sixty-two years. They were not perfect, but they were a hard-working, God-loving couple who created a safe and loving environment for Sandra and me.

It all started in Kannapolis, North Carolina. When the boll weevil ate the cotton crop in Georgia, my father's family moved from the farm to work in the textile mill in Kannapolis. At that time, Kannapolis was the largest unincorporated town in North Carolina. Cannon Mills owned the entire town. They owned and rented out all of the "mill houses." They owned all of the stores and provided the police and fire protection for the community.

It was there that Sam and Grace met and fell in love. In 1935, at the ages of twenty-three and twenty-five, they eloped to South Carolina, where they were married. None of their parents were aware that they were married. For three months, each continued to live with their parents until they got enough money to rent their own house. Years later, I asked my mother, "Did you have sex during this time?" To which she responded, "No, not until we got our own place." (Life was different in the 1930s.)

The doctor told my mother that she probably would not be able to have children. But she prayed, and one year later, on January 10, 1938, I was born. Four years later, my sister was born. Mom was always grateful for her children, and once I heard the doctor's prediction, I always sensed that God had a hand in our births.

At the age of two, I moved with my parents to a new house that they had built in China Grove, four miles north of Kannapolis. (Not the China Grove that the Doobie Brothers sang about.) It was named for the chinaberry tree, of which there were groves. All of my childhood memories center around this house, which cost $5,016 brand new. And it had indoor plumbing. (Life was different in the '30s.)

Then came the war (World War II). My father's brother had moved to Syracuse, New York, to work in a steel mill. The word was that if you worked in a "defense plant" you would not be drafted into the military. My dad decided he would rather

work in the steel mill than dodge bullets. So we moved to Syracuse. We were only there for eighteen months. My only memory is that in the winter, the snow was taller than I was. After
the severe winters, my dad decided he would rather be in the
military, whereupon he moved the family back to China Grove,
and he joined the Navy.

For the next three years, Mom was the solo parent. She wrote
Dad a letter almost every day. He was on board a ship without
daily mail deliveries. He later told us that sometimes he received
a bundle of letters, but he eagerly read each one. Periodically
we would receive a letter from Dad. I remember listening as
my mother read his letters to Sandra and me. At the end of the
letters, he would almost always say to us, "Give your mother a
big hug for me and remember to obey her."

Our house was the third house on the right on the one-lane
dirt street that ended at the railroad track embankment. The
houses were close and the neighbors were friendly. My grandfather lived in the first house with my grandmother, who was
bedridden, and their daughter, Reba Nell, and her son, Kinney.
My Uncle Bob and Aunt Hazel lived in the second house. They
had two sons, Bobby and Darrell. We often played backyard
basketball behind their house. On Saturdays, young men from
the Black community half a mile away would come and join us.
(These were the days of racial segregation.) We always enjoyed
playing together, but when the game was over, they went back
to their community, and on Monday, they went to their school,
and we went to ours. (Things were different in the '40s.) But
here the seeds were planted in my mind that all men are created
equal. These seeds would continue to grow in the coming years.

Behind the house was a large garden space where I learned

to plant potatoes, corn, green beans, squash, cucumbers, tomatoes, turnip greens, and peppers. From my earliest memories, I helped my dad with the garden every spring and summer. Mom's job was to cook and can all that the garden produced. (This was before freezers.) Work was a part of my life, which, I am sure, impacted my own work ethic, which has served me well. I have never viewed work as a chore but as an opportunity to be productive.

To the left of the garden was a "car shed" big enough for one car and with two storage rooms on the side closest to the garden. One was used to store coal, which we burned in the stove to keep warm in the winter. The other stored our tools for working in the garden and mowing the grass. The plow was a "push plow," and the lawn mower was a "push mower." That is, your pushing provided the power. (Life was different in the '40s.)

Behind the car shed was the chicken lot where we always kept a least a dozen hens and one rooster. I often fed and watered the chickens and gathered the eggs. We had lots of deviled eggs and egg salad sandwiches. Behind the chicken lot was the pigpen. We had only one pig, and after he reached "eating stage," he was made into sausage, pork chops, and lard. I don't know why, but we never had another pig. I was elated because I never liked "slopping the pig."

My routine during my school years was to come home and eat a snack then do my homework. After that, in the spring and summer, I would help Dad with the garden. When I got older, I would mow the grass on Saturdays. As for work inside the house, my sister and I shared the task of washing dishes after the evening meal, a job I still enjoy doing. I like the sense of accomplishment that comes from filling up the dishwasher and then washing the pots and pans in the sink. Of course, in my childhood, we did not have a dishwasher. We washed everything in the sink and put it on a plastic tray to dry. This skill has served me well in my marriage, since my wife, Karolyn's, love language is acts of service. "Thanks, Mom, for teaching me how to wash dishes. You made a great contribution to the success of my marriage."

When it got too cold to work in the garden or play outdoors, Sandra and I would play indoor board games together. Once or twice a week, as a family, we would listen to the national news on the radio. Then sometimes we could listen to one other radio program. The only ones I remember are *The Lone Ranger* and *Life with Luigi*. The latter was a situation comedy about the experiences of Luigi, a newly arrived Italian immigrant in Chicago. We would laugh together as a family. Those are still pleasant childhood memories.

Now if you are wondering, television had not yet come to our street. In 1946, only six thousand homes in the United States had television sets. That number rose to twelve million by 1951. By 1955, half the homes in America had television sets. Of course, it was all black and white; color came later. The first neighbors on our street to get a television were Uncle Bob and Aunt Hazel, who lived next door. That was 1951. I was thirteen years old. I remember the first time I visited and saw television. It was hard to believe that we were seeing people in other parts of the country!

As I remember, it was 1953 before we had a television set in our house. We mainly watched CBS News and the local news, which came out of Charlotte. I graduated from high school in 1955, so television did not play a major role in my childhood.

I have often wondered how my life would have been influenced had I been raised with television and computers. I know it sounds like an old man talking about "the good old days," but I'm grateful that my childhood was filled with study, work, play, and church. I was not troubled with the trauma of world news, which now flows steadily into American homes. I was always busy doing the next thing.

To the parents who may be reading, let me encourage you to build structure into your child's life. Children thrive in a structured lifestyle. By structure, I mean a time for study, play, work, entertainment, and sleep. In my years of counseling, I have learned that children who simply do what they want to do, when they want to do it, are often bored by the time they get to be teenagers. Children need guidance. They do not know what is best for them. Parents are older than their children and, for the most part, have more wisdom. Having a structured lifestyle gives the child a sense of security. Don't allow your child to spend all of their free time watching a screen or playing video games. Such a lifestyle will follow them into adulthood, and it will not be beneficial to their wellbeing.

Let me emphasize the value of a set bedtime for children. I am amazed when I walk into Walmart at 9:30 p.m. and see four- and five-year-old children shopping with their parent. Even if you are a single mom, I would encourage you to establish a set bedtime for your children. Children need regular sleep patterns. Their physical and emotional health is adversely affected when they do not get adequate sleep. A set bedtime for the children is also beneficial to the parents. It gives them time to get special projects completed or to relax and enjoy time together.

Another important goal for parents is to teach the children

life skills. I would never have known how to plant and tend a garden if my father had not taught me. Recently, I was having dinner with a group of professional football players and their wives. In the course of our conversation, we talked about what happens when they "age out" of football. One of them said, "Our problem is that we don't know how to do anything except play football. Since I was a child, football has been my life. I don't know how to do anything else." The others chimed in affirmation. I suggested that they make a list of all the things they would like for their children to be able to do by the time they are eighteen years old. Then at the appropriate age, teach them those life skills.

For years I have made this recommendation to parents. If you have teenagers, let them help you make the list. You might be surprised at what they suggest. There is an ancient Hebrew proverb that says, "Train up a child in the way he should go; even when he is old he will not depart from it" (Prov. 22:6 ESV). If as an adult, your child gets married, their spouse will praise you for how well you equipped your child for life.

At the Schoolhouse

When we moved back to our house in North Carolina, I was six. In Syracuse, I started the first grade at age five and a half, so when we returned to North Carolina, I had finished half of the first grade. Mom and the school administrators decided I was ready for the second grade. Thus, I was always a year younger than most of my classmates, graduating from high school at the age of seventeen. Every morning, I would walk to the bus stop located at the intersection of highway 29-A and Mt. Moriah Church Road, where I would ride with the neighborhood gang to Landis Elementary School. I caught the same school bus through elementary, junior high, and high school, which were all located at the same site, near the Landis textile mill.

Memories of my educational experience are pleasant, except for fifth grade. That's the year that I got a spanking from Mrs. Coffee. I don't remember what I did, but I have never forgotten the pain of the paddle she used. (Life was different in the '40s.) Other than that, school was enjoyable. I always enjoyed reading. In elementary school, my favorite series was *Silver Chief: Dog of the North*. I could almost see the breath of the dogs and feel the chill of the air. Maybe this is where the thrill of adventure was born in my mind.

In junior high (today's middle school) and high school, I enjoyed basic math but never got excited about algebra and geometry. Physics and biology were my favorite science classes. English was my favorite subject—both grammar and literature. But my favorite class was Introduction to the Bible. That's right, Bible was taught in the public high school. (Life was different in the '50s.) Miss Jabour was my Bible teacher, and she had a deeper impact on my life than she ever realized. In fact, it was her comment that later took me to Chicago and the Moody Bible Institute. But that's a later story.

One tragic event touched me deeply in high school. The county built a new high school building. In the process of construction, there was an explosion, and one of our janitors was killed. I never thought much about death until that event. I felt sad that someone's father and husband was now dead. I did not know him personally, but I felt the pain. I also reflected on the reality that life is temporary. Death can be sudden.

That was my first exposure to grief. Through the years as a pastor, I have stood by many open graves and have learned why Jesus wept by the grave of Lazarus (John 11). I don't think He was weeping for Lazarus, because He knew that He was going to bring him back to life. I think Jesus was looking down the hallway of the future and identifying with the pain that death brings to the human heart. I have learned to "weep with those who weep" (Rom. 12:15 ESV).

My senior year, I was elected class president. I often wondered why because I did not see myself as a leader. When it came time for the class to vote on "best this" and "best that," I received five superlatives. We were only allowed to have two, so I chose "friendliest" and "most likely to succeed." Those two seemed to go together in my mind. At the age of seventeen, I went to college in Illinois and never returned to live in China Grove. So I never kept up with my classmates. I've often wished I had made a greater effort to stay connected.

At Church

There was another major influence in my first seventeen years—church. Landis Baptist Church, where pastor Arthur Blackburn, my Sunday school teacher, Bertha Cranford, and my youth leader, Elmer Phipps, all had a profound impact on my life. Church was a major part of life for our family. We attended Sunday school and worship every Sunday morning. We went back to church on Sunday evenings and Wednesday evenings. In high school, our youth group was a big part of my life.

My dad did not become a Christian until after he and Mom were married. Mom was a Christian and regular church attender. Dad started going to church with her when they were dating. (Don't underestimate the influence of a young girl on a young man.) Dad became a true follower of Jesus about two years after they were married. When Mom was older, I said to her, "Mom, you were taking a risk when you married Dad before he became a Christian." "I know," she said, "but God took care of that." She was right because when Dad committed his life to Christ, he was "all in" from that time forward.

One decision my dad made illustrates his commitment to the biblical teaching on the importance of the father's role in the life of children. The textile mill had three work shifts: first shift, 7:00 a.m.–3:00 p.m; second shift, 3:00 p.m.–11:00 p.m.;

third shift, 11:00 p.m.–7:00 a.m. Dad chose the third shift. Why? Because he wanted to be at home in the afternoon and early evening when my sister and I were at home. So, he worked all night and slept each day until 3:00 p.m. Therefore, he was ready to be with us for those afternoon and evening hours. Of course, this also enabled him to work in the garden each afternoon. Since I was his "helper," it instilled within me the joy of working and seeing the results of hard work. It also allowed us to have dinner together as a family each evening, a tradition Karolyn and I emulated when our children were at home.

It was at church that I first realized that I was not a Christian. At the age of ten, I was sitting in church one Sunday evening. As the preacher gave his sermon, for the first time in my life, I realized that I had never consciously accepted Christ as my Savior and Lord. I knew the Bible stories, but I had never sensed God asking me to let Him into my life, to give my life to Him, and to let Him guide my life. I was deeply aware that God was calling me, but I was afraid to step out in front of all the people and acknowledge that I was not a Christian.

> While I obviously did not know the depth of what that decision would mean, I knew that God was calling me, and I responded.

I think many people have the idea that if they go to church regularly they are Christians. That night, I knew in my heart that was not true. There was more to it than that. There had to be a personal response to Christ.

I struggled with the thoughts and emotions that I was experiencing, but I did not respond when the pastor urged anyone who wanted to become a Christian to step out and come to the front of the church. I walked out that night feeling I had rejected God. I promised myself that I would do it next Sunday. However, when I sat in the service the next Sunday, I did not feel anything like I had felt the Sunday before. I wondered if I had missed my chance. I knew God had called me, and I had resisted. So I again walked out feeling troubled. The following Sunday, I was back in church, and at the end of the service, I again felt the call of God to give my life to Him. This time, I almost ran to the front of the church when the pastor gave the opportunity. That night I gave my life to Christ—the greatest decision I ever made.

I know that many adults wonder if children really understand what they are doing when they express the desire to follow Christ. While I obviously did not know the depth of what that decision would mean, I knew that God was calling me, and I had responded. What I have come to know as the "peace of God" settled on my heart that night, and I knew that I was a true Christian. That decision has influenced every other decision I have ever made.

The test of my commitment came about two weeks later when one morning at the bus stop, Bo Gulledge, a senior in high school, walked up to me and said with a snarl in his voice, "Someone told me that you are a Christian. Is that true?" I looked up at his white T-shirt with a pack of cigarettes rolled up in his sleeve, and I was speechless. "Well, are you?" he yelled. "No, not me," I said. "Well, good," he said as he walked away.

My heart was broken. I remembered the story of Peter denying Jesus three times. I felt like I had failed God, just like Peter. That night I cried when I prayed and asked God to forgive me and to help me to never deny Him again. Bo never approached me again, and I kept my distance from him after that. I have often regretted that I did not go to him and set the record straight about my commitment to Christ. Bo graduated that year, and I never saw him again. Years later, as an adult, I was visiting China Grove and asked several people if they remembered him, but no one did. I've often wondered, "What ever happened to Bo Gulledge?"

That painful experience left a deep mark on my life. It motivated me to be open and honest about my spiritual beliefs; not belligerent, not self-righteous, but deeply grateful for what God has done for me and willing to share His gospel with others.

It was also in China Grove that I made my decision about alcohol. My grandfather was an alcoholic. After his wife died, his lifestyle became very simple. He worked in the mill on the first shift. Then he would come home and eat dinner and head out to Goat Turner's gas station located about half a mile on the left going south on Highway 29-A. This was the local "beer joint." He and his buddies would sit around talking and drinking until around eight o'clock, and then he would walk home and go to bed.

One night a man knocked on our back door and told my father that his dad was lying in a ditch beside the highway drunk. It was a cool evening, so my father said to me: "Get your coat on, and let's go help your grandfather." In my memory, I was around eleven or twelve years old. When we found him, he was indeed lying in the ditch mumbling. Reaching down and taking his father's arm, my dad said, "Get up, Dad, and let's go home." I got on one side and my dad on the other, and we held him upright and walked him home and put him in bed. All the while he was mumbling about not needing our help.

That is the night I decided not to drink alcohol. I don't know that my father said anything to me about it, but he didn't need to. I saw for myself where alcohol abuse leads, and I wanted nothing to do with it. It was a decision I have never regretted nor recanted. Through the years, I have seen so many young lives ruined by alcohol and drug abuse.

Which leads me to the day I decided not to destroy my life with drugs. We were playing basketball in the backyard when we heard the sound of a motorcycle. We looked toward the highway and saw a motorcycle literally flying through the air. He had come down Mt. Moriah Church Road, where we caught the school bus, crossed over Highway 29-A, and off a three-foot embankment into an open field not more than a hundred yards from where we were playing.

We all ran to the scene to hear the man screaming with pain. He and the motorcycle were enmeshed. We tried to talk with him, but he was hurting too much to listen. One of the guys ran back to the house and called the police. (This was before cellphones. All phones were connected to houses.) Soon the police and ambulance arrived and took control. We watched as they took him away.

The next day, we learned that the young man was on drugs. I never heard whether he lived or died, but that is the week that I decided never to take "mind-altering" drugs—a decision that I always seek to impress on the minds of young men. One of the great tragedies of our culture is the number of young men who are hooked on drugs before they are eighteen years old. Research has made us aware that the human brain is not fully developed until the age of twenty-five. How sad to distort the brain with drugs.

In the book *Choose Greatness: 11 Wise Decisions That Brave*

Young Men Make, a book I wrote with Clarence Shuler, we encourage young men to choose to live longer and happier by avoiding drugs and alcohol. I believe this is one of the most important decisions a young man can make. I am deeply grateful that I made this decision when I was young. I have discovered that a healthy brain is a great asset in life.

Lessons Learned in the Neighborhood

The kids who lived on our dead-end dirt street often played together in our backyards. My cousins Bobby, Darrell, and Kinney, along with Sandra and me, all lived in the first three houses. Then there was Vickey, who lived next door, and down the street was Mickey. Mickey was bigger than I was but a bit younger. I remember once when the guys all got into a chinaberry battle—shooting chinaberries with a slingshot. The berries were about the size of a marble and almost as hard. We hid behind trees and tried to shoot each other.

I hit Mickey near the eye, and of course he ran toward home crying. His older sister came out of the house, realized what had happened, and declared verbal war on us. "No more chinaberry battles!" she decreed. I felt bad about hurting Mickey. Until that happened, it was just a game. That is when I learned that if what I consider a game hurts other people, it is no longer a game I wanted to play.

Halloween also taught me a similar lesson. On Halloween night, the kids on the street would always go trick or treating. I remember once when no one came to the door when we knocked, we decided to let the air out of one of the tires of the lady's car. The next morning when she came out to drive to her job, she was furious. Someone, I don't know who, told her that I was involved, and she told my father. That is one of the few spankings I remember getting, but I never forgot it. That was the last time I ever pulled that prank.

On another Halloween, we boys all decided that if we all pushed hard, we could topple Mr. Lipe's outhouse. He and his wife never gave us a treat, and this was our "trick." Theirs was the only house on the street that still had an outhouse. The rest had indoor plumbing, which of course included a toilet. As you can imagine, all of our parents were extremely embarrassed by our actions, and each declared that there would be no more "tricks" on Halloween. We could knock on doors and accept treats, but tricks were now outlawed.

These kinds of experiences taught me that having fun at someone else's expense is not an act of love—a lesson I'm glad I learned as a child.

The Decision That Changed My Life Forever

I was a senior in high school when I had a growing sense that God wanted to use my life for ministry to others. I knew that I was going to graduate, and I wondered, "What do I do now?" As I pondered that question, I knew that God had plans for my life. So one Sunday I asked a few friends of mine if they would join me for prayer that afternoon. I wanted them to pray with me that God would give me wisdom regarding His plans for my life. By the end of that prayer time, I knew that God wanted me in vocational ministry.

I only knew of two "spiritual vocations": pastors and missionaries. I imagined missionaries working in the jungle, and I really did not like snakes, so I figured that God wanted me to be a pastor. That afternoon, I gave my life totally to God. I wanted only to do what He wanted me to do. There was a sense of relief and excitement. Relief from the burden of "What do I do now?" And excitement about what lay ahead.

Yes, the first seventeen years of my life had a profound impact on life lessons learned.

THINGS I LEARNED FROM CHILDHOOD

1. That loving parents greatly enrich the lives of children.
2. That having fun at the expense of others ceases to be fun.
3. That discovering the joy of reading books prepared me for my educational journey.
4. That being involved in a loving church had a profound, positive impact on my life.
5. That alcohol and drugs destroy lives.
6. That hard work pays huge dividends.

The Powerful Influence of My Educational Journey

1955–1967

Life in the City

CHICAGO:
MOODY BIBLE INSTITUTE

The next decade of my life was dedicated to higher education. As I said, it all began in Miss Jabour's Bible class my
senior year in high school. She mentioned Moody Bible Institute in Chicago. I had never heard of the school. Jerry Wright,
a friend of mine, wrote for and received a school catalogue.
One day in study hall I borrowed and read it. By the time I
finished reading, I knew that was the school I should attend. So
I wrote for a catalogue and application form. (This was before
the days of computers.)

As I filled out the application, I noted that I needed a letter of
reference from my pastor. So I asked him what he knew about
Moody Bible Institute. He said, "I know it is in Chicago, and
I know it was started by an evangelist by the name of D. L.
Moody. He was the Billy Graham of his day in the 1800s. That's
about all I know." (I realized that I knew more about the school
than he did.) "Would you be willing to write a letter of recommendation for me?" I asked. "I want to go there." "I would be
happy to," he replied.

A few months later, I found myself on a Trailways bus in Salisbury, North Carolina, on my way to Chicago. I looked out the window at my mom and dad. Mom was crying. I assumed she was happy, but I did not dwell on her tears. I was afraid that if I did, I might start crying. (Of course, I knew nothing about the mixed emotions that parents feel when they send their children off to college.)

I don't remember much about the long bus ride. What I do recall is arriving in Chicago, taking my two suitcases, and walking to the street and waving my hand at a taxi driver. I had never ridden in a taxi, but I had seen people on television flag down a cab. I asked if he could take me to Moody Bible Institute. In a few minutes, I arrived at 820 North LaSalle Boulevard, paid the driver, and walked through the Arch onto the campus of Moody Bible Institute. Little did I know that my world was about to radically change.

Since the boys' dorms were full, I was assigned to live at the Lawson YMCA two blocks from the Institute. Moody had leased the fifth floor as additional space for young men. So I rolled my two suitcases down Chicago Avenue and looked up at the high-rise YMCA building. Living with a roommate from Iowa, I did something I had never done—learned to share a room with someone else. It was also at the YMCA that I learned to swim. I had never been to a swimming pool. (Life was different in the '50s in small-town North Carolina.)

I will never forget that first winter. The two-block walk from the YMCA to Moody seemed like a mile as the cold winds from Lake Michigan blew against my body. Fortunately, once I got to Moody, I did not need to go outside again until the evening when I walked back to my room. Moody had underground tunnels to all the buildings on campus. I am deeply grateful to the person who made that decision.

Moody's curriculum was organized around vocational goals. There was the pastors course, the missionary course, the music course, the youth ministers course, and so on. Moody was a training school for students who felt led to pursue Christian ministry. Obviously, I chose the pastors course. The next three years, my life was filled with courses designed to train young men to be pastors. I studied Old Testament Survey and New Testament Survey. Then we had in-depth courses on individual books of the Bible. I studied Greek, hermeneutics, and homiletics. (I had never heard of these words.) In fact, I was exposed to many things I had never heard of before. It would be an understatement to say that my mind and heart were greatly expanded by my studies at Moody.

It was at Moody that I learned there were Christians who were not Baptists. (Go ahead and laugh.) In my small town, we did have a Methodist and a Presbyterian church, and I had heard about Pentecostals, but in my mind the Baptists were the real Christians. At Moody, I met students who had labels I had never encountered. I came to realize that the Christian family is much larger than I ever imagined. What really surprised me was that we all seemed to be more similar than different. We were all committed to Christ as Savior and Lord. We all wanted to follow His plan for our lives.

I also learned much outside the classroom. Each student at Moody had a Christian service assignment each semester. Every week, students were scattered across Chicago involved in various ministries. I worked in jails, hospitals, boys' clubs, rescue missions, and more. The objective was to give students practical experience in ministry, not just classroom studies. I still have vivid memories of these opportunities to serve in the "real world." I am deeply grateful for the impact these experiences had on my life.

One memory that stands out is helping with an afternoon Sunday school for inner-city children. As students, we walked the neighborhood, from apartment to apartment, gathering children and walking them to our meeting place. Then we would teach them stories from the Bible and what we could learn from those stories. For those who were old enough to understand, we taught them how God loved us so much that He sent Jesus to show us how much He loved us. We explained the good news that because of Jesus' death and resurrection, we could become God's children and live forever with Him. I have often wondered what happened to each of those children.

I am reminded of the story that Jesus told about planting seeds. Some seeds fell along the path and were trampled; others were eaten by birds; others fell on the rocks and among thorns. But some fell on good ground and yielded "a hundred times more than was sown" (Luke 8:8). I hope that some of our gospel seeds fell on "good ground" in the hearts of those children. Only heaven will reveal the fruit of our seed planting. This side of heaven, we will never know the full results of our efforts to love others as Christ has loved us, but I have learned to leave the results to Him and rejoice in the privilege of sowing seed in His name.

It was at Moody that I learned to have a daily "quiet time" with God, to sit with my Bible and ask God to bring to my attention what I needed to hear from His Word. I developed the pattern of reading through the Scriptures a chapter each day listening to God and seeking to apply the Scriptures to my life. Nothing has impacted my life more than this daily time with God. It is a practice I have followed through the years. Yes, I talk with God throughout the day, seeking His wisdom in whatever I am doing. But in my mind, there is no substitute for my "sit-down" time with God each morning.

Another lesson I learned is that forgiveness does not remove all the consequences of wrongdoing. The professor had given us a test, and the following class, he handed out our test and asked us to grade ourselves. He went over each question and gave the correct answer. We were to give ourselves a check if we had answered correctly and an X if we did not have the correct answer. One question involved writing from memory a particular verse from the Bible. I don't remember the verse, but I do remember that I missed one word. I had written a "that" when it should have been a "which." The professor stressed that the quote had to be exact in order for each of us to give ourselves a check. I thought, "Who cares if it is a 'that' or a 'which'? I got the verse correct."

Later that afternoon I was plagued with the reality that I had given myself a check when it should have been an X. I could not shake the guilt. So I got on my knees beside my bed and, with tears, admitted to God that I had sinned. I arose knowing that God had forgiven me. If there is one thing the Bible teaches clearly it is that God will forgive anyone who confesses sin and asks for forgiveness. That is the central message of the Bible. Christ paid our penalty on the cross so that God could forgive us and still be righteous and holy.

Knowing that God had forgiven me, I also knew that I had to confess my failure to my professor. The apostle Paul said about himself, "I strive always to keep my conscience clear before God and man" (Acts 24:16). I had made my peace with God—now I needed to take the second step. I went to the office of my professor and told him what I had done. He thanked me for being willing to admit my failure and told me that he was certainly willing to forgive me. Then he said, "Now, I will have to take this to the ethics committee and let them decide what should be done." That statement sent me into shock. I'm thinking, "What does this have to do with the ethics committee?" But of course, I said "okay" and walked out of his office.

A week later, I was informed that the committee had decided to give me a zero on the entire exam. My first thought was, "This is unfair. I made things right with God and the professor. Why would they want to punish me?" I wrestled with the question, "Does it really pay to be honest?" It took me a few days to work through my emotions, but I eventually realized that forgiveness does not remove all the consequences of sin. The Bible is filled with examples of this reality. Follow the life of King David in the Old Testament, and you will see this played out in his life.

I have never forgotten this (hard) lesson. Over the years in my counseling ministry, I have been able to help couples realize that when we fail each other in marriage, we need to confess our failures and forgive each other. However, forgiveness does not remove all of the consequences of our failure. Yes, a wife may genuinely forgive a husband who has had an affair, but forgiveness does not restore trust. Nor does forgiveness remove the emotional pain in her heart. Trust must be regained over time as he chooses to be trustworthy in the future. Emotional healing takes time and an understanding husband who does not tell her that she needs to "get over it."

This lesson, learned as a young student, has served me well. It has become abundantly clear that when God says, "Don't do that," He speaks out of love. When He says, "Do this," He also has my well-being in mind. All of God's words to us grow out of His love for us. Some Christians have the idea that sin is no big deal. They reason that we just ask God to forgive us, and all will be well. They fail to consider that sin always has negative consequences. We are never better for having sinned.

I learned another lesson walking down Dearborn Street in Chicago. I had a part-time job at the Merchandise Mart, a large building not far from campus, in the afternoons. My walk down Dearborn was filled with enticing photos of women, and here and there, a woman would be sitting near her window and inviting men to come inside. With my young male hormones raging, I struggled with temptation. One night I cried out to God and said, "Please deliver me from this temptation." Immediately, there came to my mind a verse of Scripture I had memorized. "There hath no temptation taken you but such as is common to man: but God is faithful, who will not suffer you to be tempted above that ye are able; but will with the temptation also

> When God says, "Don't do that," He speaks out of love.

make a way to escape, that ye may be able to bear it" (1 Cor. 10:13; in those days, I memorized in the King James Version). So I said, "Oh God, show me the way to escape." Immediately there came to my mind an idea that had never crossed my mind: "Walk down Wells Street instead of Dearborn Street." At that time, Wells Street was lined with the blank brick walls of old, dilapidated buildings. Nothing tempting about that. So I changed my route to work. I had literally discovered "the way to escape."

Again, this is a lesson I have never forgotten. There is always a way to escape from yielding to temptation. It is our responsibility to ask God to show us the way. He is skilled at pointing His people in the right direction. In His power, we can "resist the devil, and he will flee from you" (James 4:7). "The one who is in you is greater than the one who is in the world" (1 John 4:4).

After my first year at Moody, I went home for the summer and worked in the textile mill on the third shift (11:00 p.m.–7:00 a.m.). As you may remember, that was the shift my dad worked. So, we both worked all night and slept during the day. It gave me a taste of what my dad had done through the years and deepened my appreciation for his role in my life.

Lessons Learned
in the Mountains
of Tennessee

The second summer, I worked at a gas station in Chicago, but after three weeks on the job, I sensed that I really wanted to be doing something more meaningful. So I went to the Student Placement office and asked if they had any Christian organizations looking for summer help. They referred me to Cedine Bible Camp in the mountains of Tennessee. It was a camp for African American young people who had been involved in an after-school Bible club during the school year and were given a week at camp in the summer. Shortly thereafter, I was on a bus from Chicago to Tennessee. It was a summer I will never forget.

I was the only White counselor in an all-Black camp. One experience stands out in my mind. I had been there a few weeks when one of the campers, J.C. Upton, came to me and said, "Now that I've become a Christian, I think I need to deal with some things in my past. A few years ago, I stole some stuff from a grocery store. Two of the young men who were with me were arrested, but I never was. I think I need to go to the store owner and confess to him and seek to make things right. Will you go with me?"

I was shocked. "You know this could mean that you will go to jail." "I know," he said, "but I need to deal with this." I did not have a car, so I said to J.C., "Let's go talk with the camp director and see what he thinks. If he thinks this is what you should do, and if he will loan us his car, I will go with you." The director said that he agreed this was the next step in following Christ and he would be happy to lend us his car.

The ride down the mountain was rather quiet. We were both aware that neither of us knew how this was going to turn out. J.C. knew where the store owner lived, so we went straight to his house, stepped on the porch, and rang the doorbell. A White gentleman opened the door and stood behind the screen door. J.C. began the conversation: "I'm J.C. Upton, and I have become a Christian up at Cedine Bible Camp, and I am trying to deal with some of my past failures. You probably remember a couple of years ago when some young men stole some things from your store. I was with those boys and also stole some things, but I was never caught. Now that I'm a Christian, I have come to confess to you and do whatever you think I need to do to make things right."

The store owner looked at me and asked, "Who are you?" I said, "I am a counselor at the Bible camp, and J.C. asked me if I would drive him down to talk with you. We talked with the camp director, and he loaned us his car."

At that point, the gentleman opened the screen door and walked out on the porch. He put out his hand to J.C. and said, "I am also a Christian, and I want to commend you for coming to me and confessing your crime. It took a lot of courage to do that. Since God has forgiven me, I want to forgive you." He hugged J.C. and they both cried. So did I. Then he put his hand on J.C.'s shoulder and prayed for him. He thanked God that he had accepted Christ. He thanked God for Cedine Bible Camp, and he prayed that God would guide J.C.'s life in the future. We talked a bit further and then returned to the camp. (Incidentally, the store owner's prayer was answered. J.C. later served as a missionary in New Guinea, and then an educator, and a pastor in Tennessee for many years.)

That is the night I learned what true forgiveness looks like. It removes the barrier and shows mercy and grace in place of our deserved punishment. That is exactly what God does for us. He pardons our sins and no longer holds our transgressions against us. That is the message that J.C. has preached all these years. That is the gospel.

The three years at Moody Bible Institute greatly impacted my life. I am forever grateful to God for leading me to the school that D. L. Moody founded.

While I was studying to be a pastor, I also took courses in missions. I was exposed to the great needs around the world. I heard missionary speakers in chapel. I attended the Saturday night prayer meeting at the home of Arthur Matthews, who had served as a missionary in China. We sang from the Inter-Varsity hymnal and heard reports from various countries and prayed for those serving in those countries. I had a growing interest in missions, and my senior year, I served as the president of Missionary Union, a student organization that focuses on foreign missions.

By the time I graduated from Moody, I was convinced that

God was leading me to the mission field. I reasoned, "Why should I stay in the United States when 95 percent of the world's population lives in other countries, while the great majority of full-time vocational Christian workers live and minister in the United States?" It seemed clear to me that even with my fear of snakes, that would be God's path for me.

Exploring Anthropology

WHEATON COLLEGE

Moody Bible Institute was a three-year school in those days and did not offer a degree. (Of course, now they offer undergraduate and graduate degrees, as well as seminary degrees.) I had learned that Wheaton College accepted credits from Moody and that in two years, I could get my undergraduate degree. So I applied and was accepted at Wheaton. There was no question in my mind that I would major in cultural anthropology, a perfect preparation for working in other countries. I learned later that was also Billy Graham's major when he was a student at Wheaton.

My two years at Wheaton were very meaningful. The first year was crammed with academics and work. I had a part-time job as a janitor at a nearby junior high school. Each afternoon, I would empty wastebaskets, sweep floors, and clean toilets. Then I would return to campus and study until late into the evening. Not much time was left for social life. I did, however, have lunch or dinner several times with Elisabeth Elliot's brother Tom, who was also a Wheaton student. This was a few years after Jim Elliot and his companions had been killed by the Auca Indians of Ecuador. He kept me abreast of Elisabeth's move to return to the Aucas and share with them why her husband and others had tried to come to their tribe. It was amazing to me, an aspiring missionary, to hear all of this. Elisabeth later wrote the books *Through Gates of Splendor* and *Shadow of the Almighty*, which capture God's hand in these events.

My second year was very different. I lived with three other students at the home of Jim and Donna Murk. Jim was the unofficial Navigators representative. He was an adjunct professor at Wheaton College, but his heart was in discipling young men. Dawson Trotman, the founder of the Navigators, had greatly impacted Jim's life. In his mind, he was headed for the mission field, when under Dawson's influence he came to believe that he could make a greater impact for God by training young men to totally follow Christ. So he and Donna opened their home to the four of us and integrated us into their family. We each had household chores, which included washing dishes, vacuuming floors, mowing grass, washing cars, and helping with their five children. All this with a view of learning to do all things as unto Christ.

Every Saturday night, the home was opened to a Bible study, which was attended by additional students from Wheaton. We worked our way through the Navigators Discipleship Program, learning how to apply the Bible to life and memorizing Scripture through the topical memory system. Jim spent personal time with each of the guys living in the house. Being part of their home gave me a living example of what a Christian family looked like. Each of the five children learned to play a musical instrument. At times the house seemed like a musical conservatory. Some of you may know that a few years later, as the children got older, they traveled as the Murk Family Singers, playing and singing in churches and concert halls across the country. I am deeply indebted to Jim and Donna for opening their home and hearts to four young college students. Their emphasis on discipleship profoundly shaped my life and ministry.

While a student at Wheaton, my Sundays were spent in Chicago at the Christian Service Men's Center. North of Chicago was the Naval Station Great Lakes, the Navy's principal training base for new recruits. After several weeks of training, they were given their first weekend "liberty," and most of them would take the train into Chicago. The center offered free coffee, snacks, and lunch, so the young recruits would flock into the center. We would spend time playing Ping-Pong, drinking coffee, and engaging in conversation. I was not a coffee drinker, but with a lot of cream and sugar, I managed to hold my own.

This was where Paul's comment about becoming "all things to all men" became meaningful to me. I had the opportunity to share Christ with several young sailors, and some of the "seed" fell on good ground. I reflected on my dad's time in the Navy many years earlier, and had the sense that I was entering a bit into that world, even though I had never served in the military. Years later, I would find myself speaking on many military bases and writing a special book for the military: *The 5 Love Languages Military Edition*. I have a deep appreciation and empathetic heart for those who serve our country in the military. I pray for them as the Scriptures instruct (see Rom. 13).

My classes at Wheaton continued to open my eyes to the needs of the world. My studies in anthropology led me to in-depth studies of nonliterate cultures, how they were organized, and the role that religion played in their lives. I was also privileged to take a course on the life of C. S. Lewis taught by Dr. Clyde Kilby. Dr. Kilby was the resident expert on C. S. Lewis's life and works. Wheaton College has the most extensive C. S. Lewis collection of books and artifacts of any college in the United States. My exposure to Lewis opened another world in my small-town North Carolina mind.

My two years at Wheaton College seemed to fly by, but my mind and view of the world was greatly expanded. I remember fondly Dr. V. Raymond Edman, the president of Wheaton at the time. I especially looked forward to his chapel addresses. I am pleased that my grandson, Elliott McGuirt, is presently a student at Wheaton. I pray that his experience there will be as positive as was mine. "For Christ and His Kingdom," the college motto, is still imprinted on my heart and mind as it is on the wall at the corner of the campus.

Lessons Learned in Colorado Springs, Colorado

After graduating from Wheaton in 1960 (the centennial class) I headed west to Colorado Springs, Colorado, for the Navigators Summer Training Program—a summer that would change my life forever. The basic format for the summer was: each trainee had an eight-hour-per-day job, a weekly Bible study, a personal mentor, and attendance at evening conference sessions. The setting was Glen Eyrie, a castle-like building dating back to 1871, surrounded by a dry "moat" and lovely grounds located adjacent to the Garden of the Gods. It is one of the most beautiful and peaceful places I have ever experienced.

It was in this setting that I learned one of life's greatest lessons. My job was to work in the print shop where they produced Navigators print products. I was assigned to run a huge paper folding machine. It took sheets of paper a yard wide and long, made several folds and ended up the size of a hand-held booklet. Having just graduated from college, I had the attitude, "I can do it." So the first morning, I was given basic instructions as to how the folder operated. The important thing was to get the right pressure on each of the rods. I worked all day and was not able to get the folds correct.

The next morning, I was given another round of instructions. Again, I worked all day and was not successful. I was beginning to feel a little embarrassed. After all, I'm a college graduate. I should be able to do this. The third morning, there were more instructions, with the same results. This went on for four days. On Friday morning, I was having my quiet time with God on a large rock in the dry moat. I read John chapter 15, verse 5 where Jesus said: "I am the vine; you are the branches. If you remain in me and I in you, you will bear much fruit; apart from me you can do nothing." The last phrase hit me like a ton of bricks, and I started weeping uncontrollably. I said, "Oh God, I can't even run a dumb folder without You." Then I said, "Please give me the ability to run this folder. I cannot do it without Your help."

I wept some more and then dried my eyes and went to the print shop. The folder worked perfectly, that day and all summer long.

I have never forgotten that lesson. I am keenly aware that without God, I can do nothing. He is the author and sustainer of my life. All that I am is because of His mercy and grace. He is indeed "the vine," and I am a branch that, apart from Him, cannot survive. I am glad that I learned this lesson as a young man. Otherwise, I might be tempted to take credit for all the good things that have happened in my life. I would not be "me" without "Him."

Exploring Theology

SOUTHEASTERN AND SOUTHWESTERN
BAPTIST SEMINARY

After graduating from Wheaton, I knew that my next step would be seminary. My heart was set on Southwestern Baptist Theological Seminary. (Remember, I belonged to a Southern Baptist church.) I planned to eventually serve with the SBC International Mission Board. So, I reasoned that I should attend a Southern Baptist seminary. However, instead of enrolling at Southwestern, I enrolled at Southeastern Baptist Theological Seminary, located in the town of Wake Forest, North Carolina. There was a distinct reason that I made this choice. Her name was Karolyn, but more about that later.

From its reputation, I understood that theologically Southeastern was much more liberal than Southwestern. (For the sake of the present reputation of Southeastern, let me clearly state that today it is a very conservative seminary.) But things were different in the '60s. In my first interview with my faculty advisor, he said: "I guess you know that the theology here is quite different from the circles in which you have been traveling." I replied, "Yes, I know that. I visited the campus last year and attended a class in which the lecture was on 'Why Paul did not write Ephesians.' So, I know that the theology here is different." He said, "Well, I hope you will be open to learning while you are here." "I certainly plan to be," I replied. We shook hands, and I walked out of his office.

Thus began my one-year journey at Southeastern. I took the first full year curriculum in the master of divinity program. It was basically a rerun of the content areas I had studied at Moody in the pastors course, but from a different theological perspective.

The campus atmosphere was different from anything I had experienced. The cafeteria was hazy with cigarette smoke, as many of the students smoked after lunch and dinner. Some of the students kept beer and liquor in their dorm room refrigerators. The conversations in the student center included slang and curse words that I was not accustomed to hearing. I really felt like I was on a secular university campus instead of a Christian seminary.

In the classroom, the theological approach was basically Barthian in nature. Karl Barth, a Swiss Reformed professor and prolific author, was arguably the most influential theologian of his day. Barth was thoroughly trained in German liberalism, which viewed the Bible not as a source or revelation from God to man, but rather a product of man's ideas about God. Such liberalism had been the prevailing perspective of many seminaries in America as well as in Europe. Barth, however, believed that there was a transcendent God who had revealed Himself supremely in Jesus Christ. He saw the Bible as man's record of God's revelation, but he did not equate the Scriptures with the "Word of God." He did believe that God could speak to man through the Bible, and at that point, it *became* the Word of God to that person. That is why it was called a "theology of the Word." Neo-orthodoxy was the label given to this school of thought. The idea is that the Bible "becomes" the Word of God when you experience God speaking to you through the Bible. The historical accuracy of the Bible is unimportant. What is important is its spiritual significance. As students, we were challenged to look for the lessons we could learn from the stories of the Bible.

One exception was my Old Testament professor. His classes were a breath of fresh air. He taught the Scriptures as the authentic, divinely inspired Word of God. It did not "become" the Word of God; it was the Word of God. I eagerly anticipated his classes.

By the end of the first year, I had applied and been accepted at Southwestern Baptist Theological Seminary. When my faculty advisor found that I was transferring, he invited me to his office. "I see that you are transferring to Southwestern, could you tell me why?" he asked. I replied, "You probably remember our conversation when I enrolled. You told me that the theological climate here was different from the circles in which I had been traveling. You were right. For example, my biblical introduction professor said, 'It is not important whether or not Jesus actually came out of the grave. The important thing is that He is the resurrection and the life.' Pure Barthian theology. History does not matter; it is only the religious significance of the biblical stories that we are looking for."

I continued, "That has been the theological approach in most of my classes. This approach is presented as the new theology and that those who do not believe it are simply uneducated. I don't agree with that. At Moody we were presented the conservative, liberal, and neo-orthodox views. The professor was conservative and gave us his reasons for being so, but we were exposed to various perspectives. To me that is education. Here, I have only heard one view, and it is presented as 'the truth.' To me, that is more like indoctrination than education."

My advisor's response was, "We don't have time to teach everything. We figure that most students got the conservative view in Sunday school. The liberal view is now waning. Neo-orthodoxy is the latest and most accepted theological perspective. We want our students to be informed on the latest theological trends." That was the perspective in the '60s at Southeastern. I knew that was not a compelling theology to which I could devote my life. (Many of my readers will know that a few years later, there was a conservative resurgence among Southern Baptists, and Southeastern Seminary is currently very conservative in its theological perspective.)

The following fall, when I arrived at Southwestern Baptist Theological Seminary in Fort Worth, Texas, I walked into a totally different world. The two seminaries were so different it was hard to believe they were in the same denomination. I remember the first Wednesday afternoon I was studying in the library. At five o'clock the lights went out, and students started leaving the library. I asked a fellow student, "What's going on?" "Oh, the library closes at five on Wednesday so students can go to church," he replied. I found out that all the churches had Wednesday night activities and students were heavily involved in local churches. Things were different in Texas.

I had realized at Southeastern that the master of divinity program was essentially the same academic program I had in the pastors course at Moody Bible Institute. So I decided to pursue the master's degree in Christian education instead. In retrospect, it was a wise decision. In this program, I was studying how to build an adult education program in the local church and how to involve adults in application of Scripture to life—how to make disciples of Christ who were seeking to live as His representatives in the world. In addition, I took all of the counseling courses that were offered. At the time, little did I know that much of my life would be spent counseling couples. God has a way of prepar ing us for roles we never anticipate playing.

While at seminary, we attended Sagamore Hill Baptist Church. Karolyn and I married two weeks before we came to seminary. (More about that later.) She was actively involved in the choir ministry under the direction of Gerald Ray. Fred Swank was the pastor and had been for thirty years. The first Sunday we attended, I observed something I had never seen before or since. The entire middle section of the worship center was filled with young students. Beginning at the front were the sixth graders; then the seventh, eighth, ninth, tenth, eleventh, and seniors—five hundred total. Yes, things were big in Texas.

The first few weeks, we visited an adult Sunday school class. Somehow, it did not seem that we should be in an "adult" class. We didn't see ourselves as adults. So we volunteered to teach a class in the college department. We loved working with college students because we were students. This experience was also a foreshadowing of a major part of my ministry several years later.

I was able to finish the master's in Christian education de- gree in one and half years since I had already completed a full year of classes at Southeastern. By this time, we definitely saw ourselves going to the mission field. The International Mission Board of the SBC required that we have two years of

I preached Sunday mornings, Sunday evenings, and Wednesday evenings. It was a baptism of fire, but I loved it.

full-time vocational ministry in the United States before they would send us overseas. So we reasoned that we should return to North Carolina to minister so we could be close to family for those two years.

I was asked to be the pastor of Emmanuel Baptist Church in Salisbury, North Carolina, in 1963. They were two wonderful years. The church had about one hundred active members. We loved the people and they loved us. I was the pastor and only staff member. Because we lived directly beside the church in the parsonage, I locked and unlocked the building, printed the bulletins, visited the hospitals, married the young couples, and buried the dead. I preached Sunday mornings, Sunday evenings, and Wednesday evenings. It was a baptism of fire, but I loved it.

At the end of two years, we talked with the International Mission Board and shared our vision of training nationals on the mission field. From my perspective, that was the way to impact a nation—train national leaders who can reach their own people. The representative of the board told us that most likely this would take place in a college or seminary in that country. He added, "It would really be helpful if you had the PhD degree." That thought had not crossed our minds. But, after prayer and consideration, we saw the value of this. I resigned from the church, and we returned to Texas to pursue the PhD program at Southwestern Baptist Theological Seminary.

In the first few months, every Sunday, I would think about the folks back at Emmanuel Baptist Church. I really missed them. I wondered secretly if they might let me fly home each Saturday and preach for them on Sunday. I knew that was unrealistic, so the thought died a slow death in my mind. We returned to Sagamore Hill Baptist Church and rediscovered our Texas church family. Karolyn got a part-time job at the seminary as an administrative assistant to one of the professors, and I worked for West Chemical Company cleaning toilets in factories within a fifty-mile radius of Fort Worth. I felt very akin to Jesus who washed the feet of His disciples. He washed feet. I cleaned toilets. That's about as close as I could get. Actually, it was a perfect job, because I could choose the days I worked to fit with my seminary schedule. So, in addition to teaching me humility, it allowed me to pursue my degree.

Each summer we would return to North Carolina so we could be with family. One summer, I took graduate courses at Duke University, and another summer, I took classes at the University of North Carolina at Greensboro. These graduate courses were transferred into my seminary course load. So I was able to advance in my academic studies, and at the same time, spend time with family. Part of our motivation for spending summers in North Carolina was that we were anticipating going to Nigeria to teach in the seminary with the International Mission Board. So we wanted to spend as much time with family as possible before we left the country.

The three years passed rather quickly, and in 1967 I received my PhD from Southwestern. We were on our way to Nigeria. (There is one more graduate degree in my educational career, but that will come later.)

Looking back over my educational journey, I always remember my father's questions. After each degree, he would say to me, "You are going to get a job now, right?" I'm sure he found it hard to understand why anyone would stay in school until they were twenty-seven when his education ended with the eighth grade. While Mom and Dad were never able to give financial support to my educational journey, I knew they loved me and affirmed me in seeking to follow God's plan for my life.

> Even at this stage in my life, I'm glad that God has not shown me what lies ahead. I am fully content to live one day at a time, trusting Him to direct my path.

For me, God's plan involved a long educational journey. Each step of the journey played a significant role in how I became me. I'm glad I did not see the entire journey from the beginning. I think I would have been overwhelmed. It was one step at a time. I had never heard of Wheaton College when I went to Moody Bible Institute. Anthropology was not a word in my vocabulary when I graduated from high school. I knew that seminary might someday be a possibility, but a PhD degree had never crossed my mind. Even at this stage in my life, I'm glad that God has not shown me what lies ahead. I am fully content to live one day at a time, trusting Him to direct my path.

For those of you who may be early in your journey with God, may I encourage you to take one step at a time? Be faithful where you are. Give your full attention to your present responsibilities and opportunities. As my wife often says, "Wherever you are, be all there!" God has a plan for your life. You don't need to see the entire plan, just the next step. Maybe you are just beginning your educational career. Commit yourself to your studies, and ask God to show you opportunities to serve others while you grow in knowledge. Make the most of your undergraduate years, and if further education is in God's plans for you, He will reveal the next step. Our plans are not always His plans. That was certainly true in my life. Remember the value of small beginnings. Upon completing seminary, young pastors have complained to me, "The church only has fifty members. I was looking for something bigger." I remind them, "Jesus only had twelve, and look what happened."

THINGS I LEARNED FROM EDUCATION

1. That God's family is much bigger than I ever imagined.
2. That vocational Christian service is broader than being a pastor or a missionary.
3. That education requires discipline.
4. That education takes place both inside and outside the classroom.
5. That success in life is not measured by our educational attainments.
6. That without God, I can do nothing.

Lessons Learned from Marriage

1961-PRESENT

The Journey
That Led to Marriage

Marriage has played a tremendous role in shaping me. Her name is Karolyn, and while we went to different high schools, we grew up attending the same church. I have known her as long as I can remember. In high school, I dated her best girlfriend. On occasion, we double-dated with Karolyn and her boyfriend. In those days, it never crossed my mind that Karolyn and I would end up together.

About six weeks into my first year at Moody Bible Institute, I got a "Dear John" letter from my girlfriend. "Chicago is a long ways from North Carolina," she wrote. "I think we should break up and each go on with our lives." I was devastated. I was very much "in love" with her and felt totally rejected. I cried and begged God to change her mind. (In retrospect, a prayer I'm glad God did not answer.) I made a futile attempt to help God out by writing a letter explaining my perspective on our relationship and asking her to reconsider, but to no avail. It was over!

I was so disturbed with this turn of events that I was having difficulty concentrating on my studies. I remember kneeling by my bed and praying, "God, I came here to study, and I'm having a hard time. You know what has happened, and I need Your help. I cannot go on like this. So I'm asking You to give me peace. Let me accept reality, and move on to concentrate on Your purposes in bringing me here."

> My immediate thought was, "Wow, how did I miss her?"

That was the turning point. I stopped looking back at what was and started looking ahead to what the future held.

And that is when Jesus' words, "Come to me, all who are weary and burdened, and I will give you rest" (Matt. 11:28) became meaningful to me. I turned my heart to God and rested in Him. My studies, part-time work, and ministry opportunities became the focus of my life for the next three years.

In my senior year, I went back to North Carolina for the Easter holidays. I went to church on Sunday morning, and there I saw Karolyn. My immediate thought was, "Wow, how did I miss her?" We had a long conversation after church, in which I discovered that she was working in Greensboro as a telephone operator. (Jobs were different in the '50s.) I also discovered that she was not dating anyone. So I could hardly wait to get back to church on Sunday evening.

After church on Sunday night, I immediately asked if I could take her home. She said, "I'm with my mother." I replied, "I'll take your mother too." I knew they did not own a car. Karolyn said rather coldly, "We have a ride." I'm thinking, "How could she have been so warm and friendly on Sunday morning and so cold on Sunday night?" So I gave her time to get home, and I drove to her house and knocked on the door. "I just came by to see if we could talk," I said. She invited me in, and we had a three-hour conversation, in which I discovered why she was so cold.

On Sunday afternoon she had talked with her best girlfriend (my old girlfriend), who told her to leave me alone, because she was "in love" with me. I shook my head in disbelief. I had not seen her or heard from her in three years. How could she be "in love" with me? I said to Karolyn, "It's your decision, but I can tell you I am not going back to her. She broke my heart once. It will not happen again." So we continued our conversation, catching up with each other. I found out that Karolyn was considering going to college. She had been working for two years, saving her money, trying to decide what her next step should be. I was thrilled to hear that she was thinking of attending a Christian college. I thought, "Maybe there is a future for us." I'm not sure she had the same thought, but I knew what I was thinking.

Thus began our three-year letter-writing relationship. This was before computers, and we could not afford phone calls. (Things were different in the '50s.) As I finished my time at Moody, Karolyn applied and was accepted at Tennessee Temple College in Chattanooga, Tennessee. So, in the fall of 1958, I enrolled at Wheaton College, and she enrolled in Tennessee Temple. Now our letter-writing romance picked up until I discovered that she had started dating another guy. I was hurt. Obviously, I was more invested in our relationship than she was. But I continued to write letters. I think I wrote twice as many letters as I received from her.

Then I found out that she was going home for the summer, and I decided that I too should go home. She went back to her old job in Greensboro, but we were together every weekend that summer. However, she was receiving letters from the guy back at college almost every day. Still, I liked this arrangement better than when I was the letter writer. By the end of the summer, she had my heart—but I wasn't sure where I ranked in her heart.

The next year, I was back to letter writing. I found out later that her college guy friend said to her, "I think Gary is going to win your heart." Fortunately for me, he was right. Later that year, her college choir traveled to Indiana for a concert. So I arranged to go to the church where they were singing. When I saw her, my heart flipped. Some weeks later, she told me that when she saw me she also had a fluttering heart. After the concert, we had a few minutes together, and I told her that I loved her. She was much more reserved and noncommittal, but warm. As for me, my heart went in orbit. I don't even remember my ride back to college that night. I was floating among the stars.

The rest of the year our letters got more frequent and intense. By the end of the academic year, she came with my parents to my graduation at Wheaton. I remember how strange and yet good it was to see her with my family. It felt right that we were all together, a foreshadowing of what was to come.

Immediately after graduation, I was off to Colorado Springs for the Navigators Summer Training Program, and she returned to her job in Greensboro. Again, we were back to letter writing. By this time, we were both serious about our relationship but realized that we had spent very little time together. Ours had been a long-distance relationship. So, I proposed an idea: what if, in the fall, I enrolled in Southeastern Baptist Seminary which was in North Carolina, and she transferred to Catawba College which was also near our home. Then we could spend weekends with our parents and each other and really see how our relationship developed. She liked the idea; however, it was too late for her to apply for the fall semester at Catawba. So I enrolled in seminary, and she went back to Tennessee and began the application process for the January semester at Catawba. Another semester of letter writing.

But then, one weekend during this semester, I drove to Chattanooga for a visit, and it was there that in a very unromantic place and with unromantic words, I asked her to marry me. I was staying with a couple from our home church who were also students. One night as we sat on the steps of their house, I asked her if she would like to move to Texas with me when I finished my year at Southeastern Seminary. She knew I was asking her to marry me. (In those days, couples did not live together without being married. The sexual revolution of the 1960s had not yet exploded.) She said she would love to go to Texas with me. There was no ring given (not until she returned to North Carolina), but we both knew that we were committed to pursuing marriage.

In January 1961, we were both back in North Carolina implementing our plan. I could hardly wait for the weekends. We filled them with long conversations, burgers from a favorite local place, and church activities. On those weekends, she came to Raleigh, where I was living, and we selected her engagement ring. I was not inclined to do that without her. Our weekends together were next door to heaven. When summer arrived, I moved home with my parents, and we spent even more time together.

As our wedding date drew closer, we had one session with the pastor who agreed to marry us. It never occurred to us that we should read a book on marriage or get further premarital counseling. On August 12, we were married in the church where we had discovered each other. Her best girlfriend (my former girlfriend) was in our wedding. They have remained friends through the years.

The Slow Road
to Unity

Two weeks after the wedding we packed our few belongings and moved to Fort Worth, Texas, and I enrolled in Southwestern Baptist Theological Seminary. The plan was that she would get a job, and I would attend school full-time. That lasted for one semester. She was working for a mail-order company processing orders and had to be on the job at 5:30 a.m. Karolyn is not a morning person. Need I say more? By the end of the semester, she had stomach ulcers. So I took a part-time job at Fort Worth National Bank, and she got a part-time job as secretary for one of the Old Testament professors at the seminary. This arrangement worked much better.

However, our relationship was not what either of us anticipated. Our differences emerged and we often argued over issues. No one told me that the euphoric feelings of being "in love" had an average lifespan of two years. Since we had dated for over two years, I came down off the "high" pretty early in our marriage, and so did she. The arguments became more heated. I remember one night it was pouring rain, and in the middle of an argument, Karolyn walked out into the rain. When the door slammed, I said, "Oh God, this is bad." And it was!

We argued about little things like how to load a dishwasher. I am an organized person. When I loaded the dishwasher everything was in the right place. Thus, everything got clean and nothing got broken or chipped. Karolyn loaded a dishwasher like she was playing Frisbee. I tried to explain to her how the dishwasher was designed. It made no sense to her. She saw my plan as a waste of time. Eventually, she said, "If it is so important to you, then why don't you load the dishwasher?" I thought, "Well, I guess I could." So I said, "Okay, I can do that, but some nights I have to leave right after dinner for a meeting." She said, "I'll be happy to load it on those nights." I'm thinking, "I know, but then I have to unload it the next morning and deal with the two spoons joined together with peanut butter and try not to cut myself on the broken glasses." But what I said was, "Okay, let's try that." We did, and I've been the dishwasher loader ever since.

Then there were bigger issues. A few years later, I observed that she knew how to open cabinet doors, but she did not know how to close them. She knew how to open drawers, but she did not how to close drawers. And that bugged me. So I asked her if, when she finished in the kitchen, she would please close the cabinet doors and, in the bathroom, please close the drawers. It was a simple request, but apparently she did not hear me.

A week later, I decided to use a visual aid. I took everything out of the top drawer, placed it on the counter, pulled the drawer out and showed her how drawers worked. I said, "This little wheel fits in this little groove. It is a marvelous invention. You could actually close the drawer with one finger." Then I took her to the kitchen and said, "Now if you get this door close enough this little magnet will close it for you." I knew she heard me that day.

Every day the following week I did my door and drawer check, and every day they were open. I said, "I don't understand you. You are a college girl, a Christian, and you can't close drawers. I don't get it." Neither did she get why I was so obsessed with closing drawers. To her it was a waste of time. I was beginning to see a theme: wasted time. So I dropped the discussions, but I was still frustrated when I came home and saw open doors and drawers.

About nine months later, I came home one night, and our little daughter, who was about eighteen months old, had fallen and cut the corner of her eye on an open drawer. Karolyn had taken her to the doctor, and here was our baby with stitches.

I was so proud of me. I didn't say a word. But inside I was thinking, "I bet she will close drawers now." My other thought was, "She wouldn't listen to me—now God is working on her." (Remember, I was in seminary.) Incidentally, I am so grateful that Karolyn forgave me for all the junk I dished out on her in those years. Can you imagine living with a man who was bent out of shape about open drawers?

But would you believe it? She still did not close drawers. Two months later—that is, eleven months into the drawer-and-door journey—it dawned on me: "This woman will never close drawers." I am a slow learner, but I finally got the message. So I went to my study desk in the library and did what someone had taught me to do when you have a problem you don't know how to solve—make a list of all your possibilities and then go back and choose the best option.

I made my list: (1) I could leave her. I had thought about that before. (2) I could be miserable every time I see an open drawer for as long as I lived. (3) I could accept that as something she would never change, and from now on, *I* could close the drawers.

I went back to analyze my options. I read number one: I could leave her. I knew that was not an option. If I left her, no church would ever call me as a pastor—and besides, it was unthinkable. I read number two: I could be miserable the rest of my life about open drawers. I said to myself, "This has gone on long enough. I don't want to keep this going." Number three was obviously my best option.

I went home and told Karolyn that she no longer had to worry about the doors and drawers. I told her that I would close them when I came home and if she needed to open them again that was fine. I would close them later. Her response? "Fine!" Obviously, no big deal to her, but that was a big day in my life. From that day to this, open drawers have never bothered me. When I walk into the kitchen, I close the doors. When I walk into the bathroom, I close the drawers. It takes about seven seconds to do both. How foolish for me to have made such a big deal out of something that could be solved in seven seconds.

It was experiences like this that helped me understand that most conflicts are not monumental. As humans we have different patterns of behavior and different personalities. Thus, we will always find areas of conflict. It was years later in my counseling with other couples that I learned there are no couples who do not have conflicts. Looking back, I wish Karolyn and I would have spent more time in premarital counseling, or at least read a book on marriage together. The euphoric feelings of being "in love" had blinded us to the reality of our humanity.

We had one hour with the pastor who performed our wedding ceremony. The only thing I remember he said related to money. He suggested that each of us should have some money that we could spend as we wish. Good advice, but woefully inadequate preparation for marriage. It was our own lack of preparation that led me later to write the book *Things I Wish I'd Known Before We Got Married*—a book that has helped thousands of couples be better prepared for marriage than we were.

Our marriage did not turn around quickly. It was commitment that held us together in those early months. Neither of us entertained the idea of divorce, but both of us were miserable. I was in seminary studying to be a pastor. I remember thinking, "This is not going to work. There is no way I can be this miserable at home and preach hope to people." One day I finally said to God, "I don't know what else to do. I have done everything I know to do, and it is not getting better. In fact, it is getting worse. I don't know what to do."

As soon as I prayed, there came to my mind a visual image of Christ washing the feet of His disciples, and I heard God's word to me: "The problem in your marriage is that you do not have the attitude of Christ toward your wife." It hit me like a ton of bricks. I remembered what Jesus said after He washed the feet of the Twelve: "I am your leader and in my kingdom, this is the way you lead." The leader serves. I knew that was not my attitude. I expected things of her. She would say I demanded things of her. And, yes, she was right. My attitude was, "We can have a good marriage if you will listen to me." She did not listen to me, and I blamed her for our poor marriage. But that day, I got a different message. I said, "Oh God, please give me the attitude of Christ toward my wife." In retrospect, it was the greatest prayer I ever prayed regarding my marriage. God changed my attitude.

Three questions made this practical for me. When I was willing to ask these three questions, our marriage began to improve.

They are simple questions: (1) Honey, how can I help you? (2) How can I make your life easier? (3) How can I be a better husband to you? When I was willing to ask those questions, Karolyn was willing to give me answers. Of course, I knew nothing about the love languages in those days. But, in retrospect, her answers were teaching me her love language. When I started responding to her answers, her attitude toward me began to change. Within three months, she was asking me those three questions.

This is where I learned the key to having a healthy marriage. When two people choose to give themselves to serving each other, they both become winners. In the early days, we were both losers. We both walked away from arguments resenting each other. But when we started serving each other, the whole climate of our marriage changed. We have been walking this road now for many years, and I have an incredible wife. I said to her some time ago, "If every woman in the world was like you, there would never be a divorce." Why would a man walk away from a woman who is doing everything she can to help him? My goal has been to so serve my wife that, when I die, she will never find another man who will treat her the way I have treated her.

I believe this is God's plan. God did not create marriage to make us miserable. God knows that two are better than one. He made us to complement each other. By nature we are egocentric or self-centered. The positive in this reality is that we take care of ourselves. We eat, sleep, exercise, and learn. However, when our self-centeredness becomes the attitude with which we approach all of life, it becomes selfishness. Our approach to life is "What can I get out of this?" rather than "How can I enrich the lives of others?" Two selfish people will never have a healthy marriage.

Love is the opposite of selfishness. Love seeks to help, to

build up, to enrich the life of the spouse. Two lovers will create a climate in which marriages thrive. The good news is that we choose our attitudes in life. By nature we are selfish, but with the help of God we can become lovers. And we can choose to love a spouse who is not presently loving us. Unconditional love is the strongest positive influence on another person. We all know that we cannot change another person, but we sometimes forget that we can influence them. This reality became personal to me when God changed my heart and gave me a desire to serve Karolyn. When I chose to love her in meaningful ways, in time, she reciprocated. After all, the Scriptures say, "We love because he first loved us" (1 John 4:19). His love was unconditional. Paul the apostle said, "God demonstrates his own love for us in this: While we were still sinners, Christ died for us" (Rom. 5:8). We were influenced by His love. The same principle applies in human relationships.

In reality we influence each other every day, either positively or negatively. When you walk into the house after coming home from work, greet your spouse with a hug, talk about your day, and ask, "What can I do to help you tonight?" you have just had a positive influence on your spouse. However, if you walk in the house and do not greet your spouse, but go to the refrigerator, get a drink, and sit down with your computer, you have just had a negative influence on your spouse. The key to a growing marriage is seeking to have a positive influence on each other. The power of influence is often overlooked by couples, to their own detriment.

That power of influence, learned in my own marriage, has greatly impacted my counseling. I am keenly aware that every couple who sits in my office will be either negatively or positively impacted by how I relate to them. If I treat them with respect and take time to listen to their perspective and have empathy for their feelings, they will likely leave with hope and be willing to continue counseling. If I come across as condemning and blaming, they are not likely to return. I am deeply grateful for this lesson learned from my marriage.

A Giant Step Forward

Karolyn and I were married for twenty years before I discovered the five love languages. We had worked through the pain of the earlier years, and both of us would say that we had a good marriage. During this time, we had two children—more about that in the next chapter. Life was extremely busy. Finishing my graduate studies and then involvement in ministry was time-consuming, but enjoyable. However, when I discovered the love language concept, our marriage took a giant step forward.

The 5 Love Languages book was published in 1992, but I discovered it ten years earlier. I had used the concept in my counseling, taught it in marriage classes, and applied it to my own marriage before I ever thought of writing the book. I knew by this time that learning your spouse's love language would greatly enhance the emotional climate in the marriage. I will never forget the first time I encountered the reality that what makes one person feel loved does not make another person feel loved.

The couple came into my office. I had never met them. I found out they had been married to each other for thirty years. The wife began by saying, "Let me share a little bit about us before we start. We don't argue. We don't have any money problems." She proceeded with several more positive comments, and I was beginning to wonder: "Did they come in to tell me what a good marriage they have?" But then, she started crying and said: "The problem is I just don't feel any love coming from him. We live in the same house, but we are like roommates. He does his thing, and I do mine. There is nothing going on between us. I feel so empty and don't know how much longer I can go on like this."

When she finished, I looked at him, and he said: "I don't understand her. I do everything I can to show her that I love her, and she sits there and says she doesn't feel loved. I don't know what else to do." So I asked, "What do you do to show your love to her?" He replied, "I get home from work before she does, so I start the evening meal. Sometimes I have it ready when she gets home. If not, she will help me. We eat, and then I wash the dishes. Every Thursday night, I vacuum the floors, and every Saturday, I wash the car, mow the grass, and help her with the laundry." I was beginning to wonder, "What does this woman do?" It sounded to me like he was doing everything. He continued, "I do all of this because I love her, and she says she doesn't feel loved. I don't know what else to do."

I looked back at her, and she started crying again and said, "He's right. He is a hardworking man, but we don't ever talk. We haven't talked in twenty years. He is always washing the dishes, vacuuming the floor, mowing the grass, or walking the dog." I realized that here was a man who genuinely loved his wife, and here was a wife who did not get it.

After that experience, I heard similar stories over and over in my counseling office. I knew there had to be a pattern to what I was hearing, but I had no idea what it was. So eventually, I took time to read several years of notes that I made while counseling and asked myself this question: "When someone said, 'I feel like my spouse doesn't love me,' what did they want? What were they complaining about?" Their answers fell into five categories, and I later called them the five love languages.

So I started using this concept in my counseling, helping husbands understand that if he wants her to feel loved, he must express love in her love language. And she must learn his love language if she wants him to feel loved. I would help them discover each other's love language and challenge them to go home and try it. Sometimes they would come back in three weeks and say, "This is changing everything. Our whole relationship is different now." Then I started using the concept with small groups of couples and got the same response. It was at least five years later when I thought, "If I could put this concept in a book, perhaps I could help couples whom I would never have time to see in my office." Little did I know that the book would have a worldwide impact, having been translated and published in over fifty languages.

However, the love language concept greatly enhanced my understanding of my own marriage. Before we got married, of course, I knew nothing about love languages. But I did know that when people gave me compliments, I felt appreciated. So what did I do when I got married? I gave Karolyn compliments. I told her how nice she looked, how much I appreciated what she did, on and on. I probably told her a dozen

> She said, "You keep on saying, 'I love you.' If you love me, why don't you help me?"

times a day, "I love you." Looking back, I remember her saying to me: "You keep on saying, 'I love you.' If you love me, why don't you help me?" Then I came back with, "What do you mean? I'm going to school full-time and working part-time. What more do you want?" Obviously, that was not a loving response, and we were off into another argument. Oh, how I wish I had known about love languages in the early days of our marriage. Things would have been much easier.

When I learned about the love languages, it was apparent to me that her love language was acts of service. All of her answers to my three questions (How can I help you? How can I make your life easier? How can I be a better husband?) were revealing her love language. So, in my response, I was speaking her love language without understanding the concept. But when I finally understood the concept and we discussed it, she started giving me more words of affirmation, and I started focusing even more on acts of service. That's why I never leave the house without taking out the trash, and she tells me I am the greatest husband in the world, which I know is hyperbole, but it still feels like love to me.

When Cancer Came

In 2012, we had an unexpected visitor enter our marriage. I will never forget the morning when Karolyn asked me to sit down—she wanted to share something with me. "I have just heard from the doctor, and he says that I have uterine cancer. He can do surgery next week, and then I will need to have chemo treatments. I found this out yesterday afternoon, but I did not want to tell you last night because I wanted you to be able to sleep."

I sat in shock for a moment. Then came the tears, first because she was thinking about my sleep and then because I knew what this meant. As a pastor, I had walked the cancer road with many people through the years. I knew the results of chemo treatments, the upside and the downside. I knew there was no assurance what the final results would be. Then I wiped my tears and said, "Okay, then here is what I am going to do. I am going to cancel all of my speaking engagements for the next year. I will be with you every step of the journey. We will walk this road together."

Her response was immediate. "Now listen to me," she said. "You are not going to cancel anything. God knew this was coming. It is not a shock to Him. He will be with me. I know you will be here when I need you, but you are going to do what

God has called you to do. If I have a need and you are away, I have friends who will be here in five minutes."

I knew she was right about that. She had many friends who deeply loved her. So I said, "Let me think about that and let's pray that God will give us wisdom." So I prayed, and we both put the situation in His hands, knowing that He would guide us on this unexpected journey.

That day, she called our daughter, who is an OB/GYN physician, and shared the news. Shelley asked when she was having the surgery and arranged to be there the day before and several days after the surgery. She helped both of us understand the medical process, and also helped us get a second opinion about chemotherapy. After examining the data, her physician friends agreed that chemo was the best option. So, in a few weeks, she began treatments.

As many cancer patients can attest, the chemo journey was not pleasant. In due time, she lost her hair, and her stomach would not tolerate food. She lost weight, and waves of pain were her constant companion. There were times when we both wondered if this was to be her doorway to heaven. Later she said, "The only thing that sustained me was the Scriptures I had memorized as a child and in college. Sometimes I was too weak even to pray, but those verses kept rolling through my mind as a reminder that God was with me, that my life was in His hands."

As a husband, it was hard to see her suffer. For the better part of a year, she only left the house for medical appointments. I would sit with her when she had the chemo treatments and pray that they would be successful. I saw the negative effects of the treatments, and hoped that there would also be positive effects ultimately. Things seemed to get much worse before they got better, but in time, the treatments were ended, and the long journey of recovery began. Little by little, her body regained weight and strength, until eventually she was ready for the wig and the hats. I think at one time she had thirty hats.

Karolyn calls 2012 her "lost year." However, she is quick to say that it gave her a new appreciation for life. I remember when she had her eightieth birthday, someone asked her if she was reluctant to share her age? She replied, "Oh no! I'm happy to say I'm still alive. I'm grateful to God for every new birthday." Both of us realize how blessed we are and seek to make the most of each new day.

My marriage to Karolyn has greatly impacted my life and ministry. I would not be "me" without her influence. She is my greatest encourager. She was an English major, so she edits all of my books. My publisher said that my manuscripts are the cleanest they receive. I said, "There is a reason for that. Her name is Karolyn." She agreed freely to let me share our own struggles in the earlier years. We both knew that if we were going to help other couples, we needed to be honest about our own journey. The amazing thing is that God uses even our hard times to make us who we are and for His glory.

> The way Karolyn handled the unexpected intruder reminded me of how important it is to walk closely with God. When the hard times come, and they will for all of us, we need His Spirit to minister to us and pray for us.

My empathy for hurting couples grew out of my own pain in the early years of our marriage. I know what it is to be married and miserable, to feel that things are not going to work out, that we are too different. I don't know if I would ever have gone into the counseling ministry if we had not gone through such struggles. But I also know what it is to find hope and healing. I know what God can do if we give Him a chance to change our hearts and attitudes. I know what it is to have a wife who is loving and supportive, and I know the deep satisfaction of being a loving husband. So, I bring hope to the counseling office.

I sometimes say to couples, "I can understand that you have no hope for your marriage. I understand how you can get there. I've been there. So, what if you go on my hope? Because I have hope for you. I know in my heart that your marriage can be different. If you will go on my hope, and if you are willing to meet with me and try some of the things I suggest, we will see what happens." Over the years, I have seen many marriages restored. This is the joy of every marriage counselor.

Yes, my marriage has been a major influence—teaching, inspiring, and shaping me.

THINGS I'VE LEARNED FROM MY MARRIAGE

1. That being a Christian does not exempt us from marital struggles.
2. That the darkest of nights can be illuminated if we turn to God for help.
3. That selfishness destroys and love builds healthy marriages.
4. That knowing and speaking each other's love language makes all of life easier.
5. That we can solve conflicts without arguing if we listen empathetically.
6. That in God's kingdom, the leader is a servant.

How My Children Influenced Me

1964–PRESENT

Learning That
No Two Children
Are Alike

No parent has ever been "un-influenced" by their children. We most often think of parents' responsibility to their children to teach, train, and influence them in a positive direction. However, our lives as parents are also greatly impacted by our children. Our two children, Shelley and Derek, have had a profound influence on me.

Shelley arrived three years into our marriage. I had finished my first seminary degree and was pastoring a church in Salisbury, North Carolina. I will never forget the Sunday morning she was born. I took Karolyn to the hospital early that morning. After an examination, the doctor said to me: "I think it will be a few hours before she delivers. So, if you want to go back to your church and preach, I think you will be back before the baby is born." In those days husbands were not allowed in the delivery room. (Things were different in the early '60s.) I followed the doctor's suggestion, and at the end of the worship service, I announced that I would not be at the door to greet people as they left, because Karolyn was at the hospital about to deliver our baby. I could tell that the ladies in the church were not pleased that I had left her at the hospital. What can I say? I was simply following the doctor's orders.

Shortly after I arrived at the hospital, the doctor came out and told me that I was the father of a baby girl. He invited me into the room, and there was Karolyn with the baby lying on her stomach. Karolyn was still under the influence of medication when she said, "It's a little girl, but I couldn't help it." In those days, parents did not know if it was a boy or a girl until the baby was born. (Things were different in the '60s.) I knew where her statement was coming from. Before we were married, Karolyn told me that she wanted to have five boys. She came from a large family: seven brothers and two sisters. The doctor said, "Don't you worry, this girl will have him wrapped around her little finger in no time." He was right about that! I was thrilled to have a baby girl.

Shelley was easy on her parents. From the very beginning, she slept through the night. In fact, it seemed like she slept most of the time. As she grew, she was a very compliant child. She basically did what we told her to do. It was fun to watch her develop motor skills, and in due time, language skills. She was a happy child, often smiling and laughing. In fact, she was so easy to raise and so much fun that I wondered, "What's so hard about being a parent? Why do other parents talk about it being so difficult?" Four years later when her brother was born, I got my answer.

Derek did not sleep through the night. In fact, it seemed that he never slept. His attitude as a child was "sleeping is a waste of time." As he grew older, he was always active, exploring everything in his environment. He was not compliant and often tested our patience. I wondered, "How could two children with the same parents be so different?" Years later, when I wrote my book *Things I Wish I'd Known Before We Became Parents*, I entitled one chapter "I Wish I'd Known That No Two Children Are Alike." I wish I had read my book before we had children. I remember the day Karolyn said to me, "I think one girl and one boy are probably enough children for us." I readily agreed. I wasn't sure I had enough energy for another child. I have always admired parents who have large families, and I've always prayed for them.

One of the things I learned from Shelley is the value of persistence; choosing a path and consistently walking in that direction. At the age of eight she told Karolyn, "When I grow up, I want to be a doctor." Karolyn responded, "Well, honey, if that is what God wants for you, that would be great." From her earliest days in elementary school, Shelley was a student. When she was in high school, she took four years of Latin and four intensive science courses. Yes, she still wanted to be a doctor. After high school, she chose a college that had a strong pre-med program. From college, she went to medical school. Then came a four-year residency and later a two-year fellowship in maternal fetal medicine. She delivers high-risk babies and loves her work. She is a model of the value of persistence.

One of the things I learned from Derek is the value of flexibility. As he grew older and observed his sister he said, "Shelley is so focused. When you focus, you miss out on so much of life." So in high school he played basketball and had his own rock band in which he played the guitar and sang. In college he had three majors: philosophy, English, and world religions.

Later he did a master's degree in expressive therapy. After working in that area for a few months, he came home and told me that he felt God leading him into some kind of ministry. He ended up attending Golden Gate Seminary in San Francisco, California. All three years, he lived in a house church in the Haight-Ashbury district and worked with kids on the street.

Later, he moved to Prague in the Czech Republic. For four years he did a similar ministry in that city. He got married in Prague to Amy who was from Michigan, but working with the ministry in Prague. Then the two of them moved to Antwerp, Belgium, and continued their ministry. For the past several years they have lived in Austin, Texas, with a ministry to the arts community. Yes, Derek knows about flexibility. His sense of adventure has led him to places he would never have gone if he had been more focused.

My life has been a combination of focus and flexibility. While I have worked on the same church staff for fifty years, I have had great diversity in my lifestyle. I am a pastoral counselor, writer, and speaker, all of which have taken me places I would never have been, and yet kept me rooted in the church. The diverse lifestyles of my two children have greatly influenced my life.

Parents Are Older
Than Children . . .
and Wiser

As parents, Karolyn and I learned along the way that children need direction. Parents are older than their children, thus we hope parents have more wisdom than children. For example, we made both of our children take piano lessons. Karolyn, who is a musician, said, "No child of mine is going through life without knowing how to read music." Shelley responded well; Derek, not so well. In fact, many times he wanted to quit. We told him that he did not need to like piano, but he had to take lessons for five years. Then, if he wanted to quit, he could. At the end of the five years, he quit. However, when he was a teenager, he wanted to play the guitar. After a few guitar lessons, he said to his mother, "Mom, thanks for making me take piano. Knowing how to read music makes learning to play the guitar so much easier."

Some parents don't think they should make their children do things that the child does not like. In my counseling practice, I have come to see that children who only do what they like to do eventually become bored. Nor do they fare well in the real world, where we often must do things that we do not enjoy. I remember when, as a teenager, Derek told me that he did not want to attend Sunday school. When I asked why, he said, "It's boring." I replied, "I can understand that. I have sat in boring classes also, some of them in school, and some in college, but I did not drop out because the class was boring. In our family, we go to Sunday school. Now you can be bored, or you can try to make it more interesting by asking questions." He started asking questions. As an adult he is an excellent teacher, and he also knows how to keep going when things are not pleasant, a skill that all successful adults will need.

One of the things I learned from my teenage children is that dialogue is much more productive than monologue. As parents, we are still the authorities in the home. We still have the final word, but we need to hear the teen's perspective. I remember once when Derek said to me, "Dad, I'm going to do what you say, but I just want you to hear me." That is when I began to recognize the power of listening. I have come to believe that parents of teenagers should listen three times as much as they talk. In fact, if we become good listeners, our teens will respond more positively to what we say. If teens do not feel heard, they are not likely to listen to what we are saying.

> I have come to believe that parents of teenagers should listen three times as much as they talk.

Another lesson I learned when our children were teenagers is the balance between words and actions. You can tell a teen how to wash a car, but they are more likely to learn by doing.

I remember when Derek was fourteen or fifteen, I would take him with me to the Juvenile Detention Center periodically on Saturday night. We would play Ping-Pong with the young men in the center. They would often share their stories with us. As we drove home, I would say, "Think about it—those young men are your age, and they are not going home tonight because they broke the law." We would talk about what might have led them to do so. These were conversations we never would have experienced if we had not gone to the detention center. Yes, I learned much about life and relationships from my children.

Shelley and her husband, John, have raised two children to adulthood: Davy Grace and Elliott, both of whom are in college. Both of whom are committed to Christ. John and Shelley are experiencing the joy of seeing their children "walk in truth." In her work as a medical doctor, Shelley has the opportunity to interact with mothers who are facing difficulties in their pregnancies. God has given her a heart of compassion and the skills to help. She has also traveled to Ethiopia to help assess the medical needs in that country and has been instrumental in helping many women there. She and John do much to meet the needs they encounter in their own community as well.

Derek and Amy likewise are deeply involved in the lives of those who live in their community. With their musical and artistic bent, they relate well to the artistic nature of Austin, Texas. With Derek's flexible past, he relates well to people in all walks of life. He, like his mother, has never met a stranger who remained a stranger. Also, because he and Amy lived in Europe for six years, they met many American missionaries and their children. They have been unable to have children of their own, but love children. So when missionary children decide to come back to the States for their college education, they often stop by Austin and spend a week or summer with Derek and Amy.

Reflections from Shelley

Recently, I asked Shelley what she remembered about her childhood. She mentioned the Friday night gatherings we had for college students at our house where they could ask questions. We did this every Friday night for ten years, when she was seven to seventeen years old. Along with college students, we had some medical students who also attended. She said that listening to their questions and the discussion that followed had a big impact on her thinking. "In fact," she said, "it was discussions with the medical students that fed my interest in medicine." She also mentioned the hiking trips we would take on Saturdays with college students in the mountains of North Carolina. "It was so much fun hanging out with the students," she said.

"I also remember the three years you were director of Camp Merriwood. I was very young, but I remember running all over the place and having fun. I especially remember the dining room," she said. As she got older, she attended our church camp for a week each summer.

This was her time away from parents. She said this helped her grow up and learn to relate to other people.

She also mentioned going out to breakfast with me once a month as she got older. "That made me feel special—just you and me together. And also the walks we took together after dinner when I was in high school. It was a time I could ask you questions. I liked that," she said. "And I loved it when you read Bible stories to me when I was little and later our family Bible reading each night. I also remember that either you or Mother would come to my bed every night, get on your knees beside the bed and pray for me. You also let me pray. I think that is where I learned to pray."

Our conversation reminded me of how impactful the parent-child relationship is. The parents take the lead, but the impact is two-dimensional. I was encouraged by our brief time of reflection on the past.

While writing this, I received the following email from Shelley: "Been thinking about childhood memories the past two weeks. Best one by far is morning Scripture reading at the breakfast table with questions for us, and application. Not sure Mom was really awake, but we were." (Remember that Karolyn is not a morning person.) "Also in middle school and high school I remember the walks around the neighborhood to talk and see what was happening. I remember our game nights each week when as a family we played games and then read stories together. These are joyful family memories for which I am thankful."

Reflections from Derek

Some time later, I asked Derek to share some memories from his childhood. He recounted some of the same things that Shelley shared; the morning and evening routines were the same for each of the children. However, he remembered that while Shelley often took walks with me after dinner, he never wanted to walk with me. He said, "Walking is dumb. You are not going anywhere. If you are going somewhere, drive." He always wanted me to play basketball with him. His love language was physical touch and the way we played basketball, it was always physical.

He also mentioned the trips that he and I made together every summer from the time he was eight years old. We began with our road trips on the Blue Ridge Parkway in North Carolina. We started in the western part of the state and worked our way up through the mountains into Virginia. Our plan was to take two days each summer. We would stop at every overlook and hike every trail. (This was the one place he would walk with me, but in his mind hiking was different from walking.) I agreed—hiking was an adventure. We would also climb the lookout towers along the way. At night we would either sleep in the car or get a hotel room. I was never into camping, nor was he. The next summer, we would begin where we had left off the previous summer. It took us four years to drive and hike the entire parkway.

Now he was a teenager, so I started asking him where he would like to go each summer. Our journeys took us to the Outer Banks of North Carolina, New York City where we met David Letterman on an elevator at the Empire State Building, Dallas, Texas, the Grand Canyon, Niagara Falls, San Diego, and Pearl Harbor in Hawaii. When he started college, we kept our tradition and each summer made a trip together. One summer we went to Oxford University in England and took a course on the life of C. S. Lewis. Another summer we went to Denver, Colorado, and took a course at Denver Seminary on "faith and doubt," taught by Dr. Vernon Grounds. Both of us reflect on the memories we made in those years.

How I Learned
to Process Anger

O ne of the greatest lessons I learned from Derek was how to manage my anger. I am not by nature an angry person. In fact, I don't remember ever getting angry until I got married. And I don't remember being super angry until I had a teenage son. I remember one night Derek and I got into an argument. He was fourteen or fifteen years old. Both of us were yelling and saying painful things to each other. In the middle of our shouting match, he walked out of the house and slammed the door. When the door slammed, I woke up. I said out loud, "Oh God, what have I done." I was crushed with my guilt. I sat on the couch and wept.

Karolyn came in and tried to console me. She said, "That was not your fault. I heard the whole thing. He has got to learn to respect you." She tried to console me, but it is hard to console a sinner. When she left the room, I got on my knees beside the couch and poured out my heart to God. "Oh God, I thought I was further along than this. How could I yell at the son I love? How could I say such hateful things to him?" The answer came back loud and clear in my soul: "Because you are a sinner." I confessed my sin to God and accepted His forgiveness. I have a profound appreciation for what God did when He sent His Son, who lived a sinless life, and then took upon Himself the penalty for our sins, so that God could forgive us and accept us as His children.

I sat on the couch and waited. I don't know how long, but eventually Derek walked back in the house. I said to him, "Derek, could you come in here, please." He sat down in the gold chair, and I apologized to him. "I want to apologize for the way I talked to you. A father should never yell at a son. I know I said some hurtful things, and that is not the way I feel about you. I lost my temper and said things that I do not mean. I love you very much, and I want to ask you to forgive me."

He responded, "Dad, that was not your fault. I started that. I should not have yelled at you. As I walked up the road, I asked God to forgive me, and I want to ask you to forgive me." With tears, we embraced each other and forgave each other. Then I said, "Why don't we try to learn to handle our anger in a better way. What if we try this: the next time you feel angry with me about anything, you just say, 'Dad, I'm angry; can we talk?' I'll stop what I'm doing and listen to you and try to understand why you are angry. And the next time I feel angry, I will say the same thing to you. Let's see if we can learn to talk through our anger rather than yell at each other." He agreed, and that was when we both began to learn how to manage our anger.

> That night was one of the saddest nights of my life, and one of the happiest. Sad because I had failed my son. Happy because I realized that he knew how to apologize.

That night was one of the saddest nights of my life, and one of the happiest. Sad because I had failed my son. Happy because I realized that he knew how to apologize. Being willing to apologize is a necessity if we are to have good relationships. I knew that someday he would likely be a husband and would need to know how to apologize. We don't have to be perfect, but we do need to deal effectively with our failures, and that involves apologizing and forgiving. That night I learned a lesson that has stayed with me a lifetime.

Years later, after helping many of my clients understand and process anger, I wrote my book *Anger: Taming a Powerful Emotion*. In this book I deal with the origins of anger and distinguish between what I call "definitive" anger and "distorted" anger and how to process each in a healthy way. I also deal with how to get rid of "long-term" anger, and what to do when you are angry at God because He did not do what you thought was right. This book has helped many individuals process anger in a God-honoring manner.

Another book that found its roots in my experience with my son Derek is *When Sorry Isn't Enough*, which I wrote with Dr. Jennifer Thomas. In this book we seek to help people understand how to apologize effectively and experience the healing power of genuine forgiveness. My own empathy with clients who struggled with anger and needed the healing that comes with apology and forgiveness grew out of my own experience with my son. So thanks, Derek, for your role in my life's journey.

Lessons Learned from My Spiritual Son — Clarence

Icannot discuss the influence of my children on my life without mentioning Clarence Shuler, one of my spiritual sons. Clarence is African American. I met Clarence when he was fourteen, and our lives have been connected ever since. I was leading a Tuesday-night youth gathering in an all-White church in the late 1960s when school integration was just taking place in the South. One night Clarence and his friend Russell walked into the gym where we were meeting. I found out later that some of our students had invited them. Here were two Black faces in the midst of one hundred White faces. With my childhood background, for which I am grateful, I had no hesitation in greeting them with open arms. From that night forward, Clarence attended the youth gatherings regularly, sometimes with Russell and other times with his friend James, and sometimes alone.

When spring came, Clarence went on a youth retreat with us. It was there, as a sixteen-year-old, he gave his life to Christ. I will never forget reading to Clarence a personalized version of John

3:16. "For God so loved Clarence that He gave His only begotten Son, that if Clarence would believe in Him, he would not perish, but have everlasting life." Clarence said, "That verse doesn't go like that." I explained that when God was talking about the world, He was talking about each one of us. Clarence later said, "I had never thought about Jesus personally loving me. It blew me away! That night I asked Jesus Christ to forgive me of my sins, to come into my life, and to make me the person He wanted me to be. From that moment, my whole life was changed. I was on a different course. I knew that I was a true Christian."

That night, Clarence became my spiritual son. Four years later, when his father died, I got to know his mother and sister. I became his substitute father. We spent many hours together in prayer and Bible study. He was an active part of our youth group. He has been a part of everything I have done since then.

Clarence later went to college and seminary, got married, and he and his wife, Brenda, have three wonderful daughters. He and Brenda live in Colorado. In 2019 he and I coauthored a book written to young men entitled *Choose Greatness: 11 Wise Decisions That Brave Young Men Make.* The thesis of the book is that the decisions a young man makes in the teen years will greatly impact the rest of his life. We are trying to help young men make wise decisions and avoid some of the pitfalls in the modern culture.

Clarence and Brenda have a heart for helping others. Brenda works in a Christian pregnancy care center designed to help young pregnant girls make wise decisions. For those who decide to keep their babies, they provide parental training and practical supplies when needed. Clarence does relational counseling with both younger and older clients. His writing and speaking have brought practical help to many.

My relationship with Clarence has greatly impacted my life. I have seen the value of long-term friendships across racial lines. I wish that thousands of Blacks and Whites could have the kind of friendship we have had through the years. From Clarence I learned what can happen when someone is willing to step out of their comfort zone and seek to learn from people who are different from them. I also learned the value of spending time to get to know each other. While in high school, Clarence came to our house every Friday night and interfaced with college students. His eagerness to learn and build friendships greatly encouraged me. I have also been encouraged as I observe how he and Brenda have invested their lives in their daughters, Christina, Michelle, and Andrea, while maintaining a ministry to other couples and youth. Clarence has written several books, and he and Brenda are speakers at FamilyLife conferences across the country. Yes, Clarence has had a significant influence on me over the course of our long friendship.

Grandparenting Is Fun

I must add that in our later years, Karolyn and I are privileged to have the joy of being grandparents to Davy Grace McGuirt and her brother, Elliott. They have brought so much happiness into our lives. Even though they do not live nearby, we have spent significant time together. They both say that one of their favorite memories is our week at the beach each summer. We have maintained this tradition since they were infants. Presently, they are both in college, but we still keep in touch. Every Sunday afternoon, Davy Grace calls her grandmother and they catch up. When I am traveling, I often send photos to Elliott of sights I think he would appreciate.

A few years ago, he and I had an unforgettable experience. I asked him, "If you could go anywhere in the world, where would you like to go?" He said, "I'd like to see the Brazilian rainforest." That caught me off guard, but I said, "That would be interesting." Two months later, I received an email from my Brazilian publisher, asking if I would come to Brazil for a speaking tour. I wrote back and said, "If I can bring my grandson, and if after we finish the tour, you will arrange for us to have two days in the rainforest, I'll come." They agreed and we did!

I still have photos of Elliott holding a baby alligator and

being hugged by a sloth. I believe that building memories with grandchildren is one of the great joys of life.

I have always been grateful that in the years when our children were at home, I made time to be with them, to have fun together, and to talk freely about life. In my counseling office, I have often encountered parents who live with regrets because they spent too much time in their vocation and too little time at home. Their children also have regrets. I remember a young adult who said to me at his father's funeral, "I never knew my dad. He was always working or playing golf. He never had time for me." I walked away with tears.

The apostle John once said; "I have no greater joy than to hear that my children are walking in the truth" (3 John 4). This is the joy I experience when I observe the adult lives of Shelley, Derek, and Clarence, and the young adult lives of Davy Grace and Elliott.

In my counseling work with so many parents whose young adult children bring them great sorrow by their poor choices, I realize how extremely blessed I am to have children and grandchildren who walk in truth and do what I have sought to do through the years—reach out in love to offer help and hope to others. There is no greater joy.

My own experience and the experience of other parents has led me to encourage parents with young children to make the most of those childhood and teen years. I have never met anyone who regretted investing time with their family, but I have met many who regret that they did not. Time with my children gave me a deep sense of gratitude that early on I learned the importance of the parent-child relationship. I was not a perfect father, but I sought to give it my best efforts and to learn even from my failures.

THINGS I'VE LEARNED FROM MY CHILDREN

1. That children are a blessing from God unlike any other.
2. That my model is more important than my words.
3. That parenting stimulated my prayer life.
4. That parenting often reveals our own flaws.
5. That good parents learn to apologize.
6. That God as our Father is the best model for parenting.

The Challenges and Joys of My Vocational Journey

1967–PRESENT

Rebounding
from Disappointment

After receiving my PhD degree from Southwestern Baptist Theological Seminary, Karolyn and I officially applied to the International Mission Board of the Southern Baptist Convention and were turned down. Our hope was to go to Nigeria and teach in the Nigerian Baptist Theological Seminary, training national leaders. The basis of our rejection was Karolyn's health. She had some rather serious physical problems, and the board said, "We cannot send you to Nigeria." As you can imagine, this was emotionally difficult for us to process. Karolyn felt that she was keeping me from going to the mission field. This thought lay heavily on her heart. Both of us were greatly disappointed. After all, this is why we had spent the last three years getting the PhD degree. Why would God have led us to do this if He knew the door would be closed? Or had the mission board made a mistake? All these thoughts ran through our minds.

In due time, we worked through our emotions without answers to these questions. I reasoned if I were not going to teach in another country, then perhaps I should teach in my own country. I applied to twenty-seven Christian colleges around the country. There were no openings. Then someone told me about Piedmont Bible College (now Carolina University) in Winston-Salem, North Carolina. I applied and was accepted.

So, in fall 1967 we moved from Durham, North Carolina, where I was serving for the summer as a youth minister, to Winston-Salem, and I became not only a professor but an associate pastor at Salem Baptist Church. Dr. Charles Stevens was pastor of the church and president of the college. At the church, I worked primarily with the youth, and in the summers directed Merriwood Christian Camp, which was owned and operated by the church. I loved working with young people. After all, I was only twenty-seven at the time.

For three years, I taught at the college: introduction to sociology, psychology, and various courses in education. I enjoyed the classroom with students, but I really did not like the more academic tasks like preparing exams, reading essays, and attending faculty meetings. I was beginning to think maybe this is why we did not go to Nigeria. Maybe this is not who I am. So when Dr. Mark Corts, the pastor of Calvary Baptist Church, a growing church on the west side of town, asked if I would be interested in coming on staff to start a college ministry and give guidance to their adult education program, I was open to the idea. I thought, "I could teach college students and not have to worry about the academic details." My PhD studies had focused on adult education with a special emphasis on how adults learn. After prayer and much thought, it seemed like a perfect fit. So, in April 1971, I became the associate pastor at Calvary, where I have remained for the past fifty years. Now I am the Senior Associate Pastor, which means I am older than any other staff member.

While I have been on the same staff for fifty years, my ministry has been varied. The first ten years, I led our college ministry (more about that later). Then I started and led our single adult ministry for ten years (more about that later). During these years I was also giving direction to our adult discipleship ministry, meeting with teachers each week to discuss not only the Scriptures but to help them develop effective teaching methods. I also started the Christian Education Institute, which offered classes for adults on various topics on Sunday evenings. I would preach when Pastor Corts was away. These were busy and fruitful years.

The past thirty years of my ministry has focused on marriage and family counseling, teaching and training lay leaders, and writing and speaking both in the church and around the world. I never intended to get into counseling, but when I started leading classes on marriage and family, I discovered that is where people were hurting. After class they would ask to meet with me privately. So, in a sense, I got pushed into counseling, and it became a major part of my ministry. Most of my books have grown out of my counseling, in an effort to help people whom I would never have time to see in my office.

On two occasions I served as interim pastor at Calvary. First, after Dr. Corts had to retire because of his health issues, I served as interim for fifteen months. Then after pastor Al Gilbert left for the North American Mission Board, I served as interim for two years, before Rob Peters became pastor. When he left, they asked if I would serve again, but at eighty years of age, I declined. There are seasons to life, and this was not the season for me to serve as interim. Each season of my ministry greatly affected my growth personally and professionally.

The College Ministry

I was super excited about starting a college ministry. In many ways, those ten years were some of the most fruitful years in terms of impacting young lives and being impacted by them. I found out that Wake Forest University, which is located in our city, offered a master's degree in anthropology. As you may remember, my undergraduate major was anthropology. So I thought, "I'll apply for the degree and, if accepted, it will give me a reason for being on campus. I will simply be a graduate student." I did and they did.

As a graduate student, I searched for a student-led Bible study. I found one and started attending. As I got to know the students, they asked if I would lead the study. I said, "I'll lead it this semester if we can agree that next semester, two of you will be leaders, and we will have two groups. I will then meet with the two leaders, and do what I can to encourage and help." They agreed. So the next semester, we had two groups. The next fall we went to four groups. The vision was now clear; each semester we would double our number of study groups. I would meet with the leaders weekly. When we got to twenty-four groups, we contacted InterVarsity Christian Fellowship, a national student ministry organization, and asked if they would send a staff member to direct our student groups. They accepted our invitation, and InterVarsity is still active on campus to this day.

It was in this on-campus ministry that I saw firsthand the power of multiplication. I had the concept in my mind from my time with Jim Murk and the Navigators ministry, but I had never seen it actually work. Thanks Jim, and all the Navigators friends, for planting the seed. You played a major role in the trajectory of my life.

In addition to the on-campus ministry, I taught a class for college students Sunday mornings at Calvary. It was composed of Wake Forest students as well as students who had grown up in our church and were now in college at NC State, University of North Carolina, Duke, Appalachian State University, and other colleges. These students came home about every third weekend. I am deeply grateful for Stan and Debbie Senft and Tom and Angel Chambers, who assisted me in this ministry. Stan was a recent graduate of Penn State University and had a heart for college students. Each fall semester, he and I would visit each of the boys' dorms at Wake Forest and personally invite them to our Sunday morning class. Tom and Angel were in charge of hospitality, providing snacks and drinks every Sunday morning. The class grew to more than one hundred students each week.

Each year I would spend twelve weeks on the topic Preparation for Marriage. During these sessions, the attendance would grow to 150. Most students think that someday they will get married. They are open to learn all they can about what makes marriage work. Many of them have seen their parents divorce, and they don't want to repeat that model.

My first book grew out of these studies on marriage. It was entitled *Toward a Growing Marriage*, published in 1979. It was designed to help singles think seriously about marriage and help marrieds discover the keys to growing a healthy marriage. That book is still in print. The revised title is *The Marriage You've Always Wanted*. This edition is geared more to those who are already married. I later wrote another book for singles entitled *Things I Wish I'd Known Before We Got Married*. This book is designed to be read and discussed by couples before they get married and within their first three years of marriage. Many pastors and counselors give this book to those with whom they are doing premarital counseling.

The third aspect of our college ministry was alluded to earlier. Every Friday night for ten years, we hosted an open house at our home. We would have from twenty to sixty students each week, many of them sitting on the floor. Our format from 7:00 to 9:00 p.m. was Q & A. They could ask questions on any topic. I was not the "answer man," but no topic was out of bounds. We would discuss openly any question that was raised. After two hours, we would break for refreshments—donut holes, and Coke or water. Then most of them would stay for another two hours, talking with each other and to us. At 11:00 p.m. we would suggest that it was time to go. These sessions made me keenly aware of the questions and struggles of college students. Providing a place where they could feel safe to ask honest questions brought me great satisfaction. As I have traveled around the country leading marriage seminars, I have often had young adult couples ask: "Do you know Lisa (or Tom) Anderson?" I would say, "Yes, they used to come to my house every Friday night." They would say, "That is my mother (or father)."

The college ministry greatly impacted my life. I knew I was touching young lives that would later influence another generation. It was here that I became keenly aware that if I were willing to express interest in students, they would freely share their inner most joys and sorrows. One of my senses today is that we are too busy to see people as individuals. We settle for surface talk and seldom really get to know anyone intimately. Some of our closest friendships started at the Friday night events at our house. For two hours after the meeting, Karolyn and I were available to listen and talk with students.

Many churches do not seize the opportunity to minister to college students. One of the deepest emotional needs of students is the need to feel that someone cares about them. Loneliness is one of the deepest emotional problems on college campuses. Students come together from all over the world and find themselves on a campus where no one knows them. Those who come from loving homes will often reach out and develop friendships, but many others bury themselves in studies, filling the mind, while the heart is empty.

> **One of life's greatest satisfactions is to have people who really know us—and still love us.**

Let me be quick to say that the need to be valued does not end when we graduate from college. Regardless of our age, we all need to feel loved and appreciated. One of life's greatest satisfactions is to have people who really know us—and still love us. Most adults have many acquaintances and few friends. Friendship begins with a single conversation that expresses interest in the other person, asking questions about their history, family, and relationships. Most people will open their hearts if they believe that the other person genuinely cares about them.

I look back on the college ministry with many pleasant memories. It greatly impacted my life.

The Single
Adult Ministry

At the end of those years, Dr. Corts asked if I would be willing to turn the college ministry over to another staff member and spend time starting a single adult ministry. He was thinking of young professionals who were now out of college and in the "real world." He said, "No one in the city has a ministry geared to single adults, and I think you are the one to do this." I was reluctant. I said, "I don't know. I love working with college students. I don't know if I want to do that." He said, "Well, think about it and pray about it." I did, for one year. I thought a lot, and I prayed a lot. At the end of the year, I agreed. We had another staff member who I thought would be able to continue the college ministry, so in 1981, I stepped into a ministry not knowing what I was to encounter.

How do you reach single adults? That was my first question. After prayer and talking with the few singles that I knew, we decided to start "A Place for Singles" on Tuesday evenings. We met in the large dining room at the church. We started with twenty-five, and within six months, we were having 150 singles every Tuesday night.

The format was simple. We had snacks available as they arrived. Doors opened at 6:30 p.m. At 7:00 I would pull the group together and give about a thirty-minute lesson on some relevant topic. Then they would break into smaller groups of nine or ten and discuss the topic I had addressed. About 8:15, I would close the discussion with prayer, and they were free to sit and talk, play board games, eat more snacks, or leave. We ended the meeting at 10:00. During this free time, I spent my time talking with those who came with questions about the topic of the evening or sharing their personal journey.

> **The need to feel loved, significant, safe, valued, and successful are human needs common to all.**

What I did not anticipate was that about half of those who attended were "single again"—separated or divorced individuals who were trying to work through their pain and struggles. Yes, the never-married young professionals were there, but those who were once married came with a totally different set of issues. The first challenge was, how do I choose topics that relate to both groups? I soon discovered that as humans we have similar basic needs—married or single. The need to feel loved, significant, safe, valued, and successful are human needs common to all. What happened was that the never-married and the single-again groups began to listen to each other in the discussion sessions. The never-married were learning about how marriage works or doesn't work from those who had been there. Each group was learning from the other. I realized that we had provided a unique space. Where else would these two groups ever interface on a meaningful level? It was beautiful to experience.

My second book grew out of this ministry. It was entitled *Hope for the Separated: Wounded Marriages Can Be Healed.* It was addressed to those who were separated from their spouse, but not yet divorced. (In North Carolina, a married couple must be separated for one year before they can get a divorce.) In my opinion, this is an excellent law. It forces them to take time to look realistically at what divorce will look like. I believe that many such marriages can be healed if the couples get the right kind of help. The updated version of that book is entitled *One More Try: What to Do When Your Marriage Is Falling Apart.* It has helped many couples find reconciliation. I would never have written that book if I had not been involved in the singles ministry for ten years. Thanks to all those singles who shared their lives with me.

The Counseling Ministry

A s noted earlier, I never intended to get into the counseling ministry. In seminary, I had taken all of the counseling courses that were offered because I knew that pastors are often expected to counsel their members. I never thought this would be a major part of my ministry. However, for the past thirty-plus years, I have listened to thousands of individuals and couples who have felt comfortable enough to share their deepest pain.

In the earlier years, I struggled with internalizing the pain they were feeling. I would go home in the evening with their stories in my mind and heart. Often I would wake up at night, and my mind was replaying what I had heard. As any counselor knows, this is not healthy for the counselor or his/her family. I knew I had to find an answer, or I could not continue counseling. So I cried out to God for help. "Lord, how do I handle this? I cannot carry this load."

The question came to my mind: "Are you helping them by carrying their pain in your heart?" I knew the answer was no. It was only hurting me and keeping me from being the husband and father I needed to be. So, with God's help, I learned how to release people into God's hands when they walked out of my office. When I was with them, they had my full attention. I listened with great empathy and asked God for wisdom in how to help them. I would pray with them before they left my office and then release them to God until our next session. I knew that I was releasing them into good hands. This was a huge lesson for me. I could not have continued counseling if I had not learned this lesson.

I have found great satisfaction in helping those I have counseled. To be a part of helping people understand themselves and make decisions that led them to productive relationships and fruitful lives is greatly rewarding. I give only one example:

Recently I visited a man who was in hospice. As I opened the door he said, "Dr. Chapman, I'm so glad you came. My wife and I are discussing my funeral, and I know you can help us." I took out my paper and pen and began taking notes as they shared their ideas. After completing our visit I said, "Well, let me pray for you before I leave." I stood up and took his left hand, and his wife went to the other side of the bed and took his right hand. I reached across the bed and took her hand.

> With God's help, I learned how to release people into God's hands when they walked out of my office.

After I prayed, I released his hand and her hand, but he held on to her hand and brought it to his face and kissed her hand. When he did, I could not contain my tears, because I remembered thirty-five years ago when they sat in my office and said, "We don't have any hope for our marriage. Too much has happened, and it has gone on for too long. We are here because a friend told us we should talk with you, but we want you to know that we don't see how we can stay together."

After listening to their story, I expressed understanding and then said to them, "I am not going to ask you, do you 'want' to work on your marriage. It is obvious that you have lost the 'want to.' So, what I want to ask is, 'Will you work on your marriage?'" (I have made this distinction with couples through the years. "Want to" speaks about our emotions. "Will you" speaks to our

> The counseling ministry kept me in touch with the real world of fractured and broken relationships.

mind. We don't choose our emotions, but we do choose our attitudes.) I continued, "If you 'will' work on your marriage, I will meet with you, and we will see what happens." They reluctantly agreed. Nine months later they walked out of my office holding hands. saying, "We never would have dreamed that we could be this happy again." Now here they were, thirty-five years later, at the end of the journey—together.

I walked out of the room praying, "O Lord, how I wish every couple could come to the end of the road like this." Not all counseling leads to reconciliation, but when it does, it brings great satisfaction to the counselor as well as the couple.

The counseling ministry kept me in touch with the real world of fractured and broken relationships. As pastors, we can sometimes slip into offering platitudes but fail to relate biblical truth to daily life. Counseling kept me rooted in reality.

The Writing Ministry

While I never thought of myself as an author, writing has become a major part of my ministry over the last three decades. Almost all of my books have grown out of my counseling ministry. Earlier I explained how I discovered the five love languages and how they greatly impacted my own marriage. Of course, I wrote the book hoping that other couples would experience the transformed marriage that so many of my clients had experienced when they discovered and started speaking each other's love language. I knew from experience how impactful the love language concept could be, but I never anticipated what would happen when the book was released in 1992.

Little did I know that for the next twenty-plus years, the book would sell more each year than the year before. At the time of this writing, it has sold over thirteen million copies in English and been translated and published in over fifty languages around the world. People have asked me, "How do you account for that?" I respond, "The short answer is God. And the long answer is God." I think what has happened on the human level is that couples read it, and it changes their own marriage, and then they want their brothers, sisters, and friends to read it. From one person to another, it has spread around the world.

When I lead marriage seminars, couples often say, "The love

language book saved our marriage. When we read it, the lights came on, and we realized how we had missed each other emotionally through the years. We took the love language profile and discovered each other's love language and tried speaking it, and it literally saved our marriage." It is that kind of response that motivates me to keep writing.

The greatest surprise was when the book began to cross cultural barriers. With my studies in cultural anthropology, I was sensitive to cultural differences. When the Spanish publisher wanted to secure the rights to publish the book in Spanish, I said to Moody Publishers, "I don't know if this works in the Spanish culture. I discovered this in Middle America. What if it doesn't work in Spanish?" They responded, "They have read the book, and they want to publish it." "Then let's go with it," I said. It became a bestseller in the Spanish-speaking world. From there it went to German, French, and other languages. In many of these countries, it has become the publisher's top bestseller.

The deepest emotional need we have on the human level is the need to feel loved by the significant people in our lives. Understanding the other person's love language helps us meet that need more effectively. When parents discover and speak a child's primary love language, they will likely see a positive change in the child's behavior. I have often said to parents, "The question is not, 'Do you love your children?' The question is, 'Do your children feel loved?'" The love language concept applies in all human relationships: family, friendships, and work relationships. Of course, love is not the only ingredient in healthy relationships, but from my perspective, it is the foundational stone.

I believe our desire for love and our desire to express love grows out of the reality that we are made in the image of God, who loves us unconditionally. I later wrote a book entitled *God Speaks Your Love Language*, in which I demonstrated that God speaks all five languages, and we tend to be drawn to His love when we see it expressed in our primary love language. Once we respond to His love as expressed in Christ, we tend to express our love to God in our own "primary" love language. It is a fascinating study of God's love and our response.

In addition to the Love Language® series, I have written on many other relationship topics that first surfaced in the counseling office. I am often asked, "How many books have you written?" My honest response is, "I don't know." Somewhere along the line, I lost count and have never taken time to go back and re-count. (The publisher says they will make sure that all of my books are listed at the end of this book. So I'm happy to let them count.) I simply stand amazed at how God has used the books to touch and change the lives of so many.

> In those early days when we were rejected by the mission board, I would never have dreamed that our ministry to other countries would be via books rather than in person.

After the success of *The 5 Love Languages*, many foreign publishers began releasing the other books also. The publishers send copies of each of the new publications on a quarterly basis. Karolyn and I will pray for the countries represented and that the books will touch and change many lives. One night a few years ago, I was opening such a shipment when I looked at Karolyn, who was sitting on the couch, and noticed that she was crying. "What's wrong?" I asked. "Nothing is wrong," she responded. "I am just remembering that we wanted to be missionaries, and now your books are all over the world."

That was one of those unforgettable moments, when we both realized that God's plans are always better than our plans and often far greater than our plans. In those early days when we were rejected by the mission board, I would never have dreamed that our ministry to other countries would be via books rather than in person.

One of my joys in writing has been to coauthor books with individuals who have had more experience than I in certain areas of relationships. Examples of this are: *Keeping Love Alive as Memories Fade: The Five Love Languages and the Alzheimer's Journey; Sharing Love Abundantly in Special Needs Families; Holding On to Love After You've Lost a Baby; Building Love Together in Blended Families; Screen Kids: 5 Relational Skills Every Child Needs in a Tech-Driven World; When Sorry Isn't Enough*, and *The DIY Guide to Building a Family That Lasts*. Entering into the world of my coauthors and learning from their experience and expertise has enriched my own life. I am deeply grateful for their impact on how I became me.

I cannot talk about my writing ministry without expressing my deep gratitude for the Chapman Team at Moody Publishers. My first book with Moody Publishers was published in 1979. Through the years, they have become like extended family to me. It is hard to believe that for over forty years, we have walked together in our efforts to enhance marriage and family relationships. Yes, all of you have played a significant role in my work and my life.

The Radio Ministry

When I was invited by the Moody Broadcasting Network to consider doing a weekly radio program, my first response was, "I don't know. I am a counselor. I don't see myself as a 'radio person.'" They responded, "What if we got you a really good cohost?" I said, "In that case, I would definitely pray about it." Two weeks later, they came back and said, "What if Chris and Andrea Fabry agreed to be your cohosts?" I said, "Then I would definitely pray about it."

I was familiar with Chris and Andrea. I knew that both of them had been radio hosts for a number of years. I had heard them and knew that they were excellent. So I said to God, "Okay, if Chris and Andrea agree, then I will take that as a sign that I should at least try this radio thing." They did and I did. We now have been working together for the past twelve years. "Building Relationships with Dr. Gary Chapman," our one-hour weekly show, has become a regular part of my life.

I am amazed at modern technology. When we record the program, I am located in my studio in North Carolina. Chris and Andrea are in Arizona, while Steve Wick is in Chicago, recording and producing the program. He is also calling our featured author of the week who often lives in another state. Steve does his magic, and on the radio it sounds like we are all in the same room except for our featured author. I always enjoy interacting with our guests, with whom we discuss important relationship topics.

Once a month we record a "Dear Gary" program. During the month, people call in and record their questions on our phone line. Chris chooses the order in which we address the questions, and I ask God for wisdom as I seek to give helpful advice. Some have asked if I listen to the questions before we record so that I have time to prepare. The answer is no, I prefer to speak from the heart. Seldom do I hear a question that I have not heard in my counseling office through the years. Of course, I also know that if I get off on a "wrong track" in my answer, Chris is there to question me and call for clarification. Now you know why I love working with Chris.

Shortly after we started our weekly program, I was asked if I would be willing to do a one-minute daily program. After prayer, I agreed, and we started recording "A Love Language Minute," for which I write the scripts. Usually, the week's programs will focus on one of my relationship books. I enjoy revisiting my books looking for ideas. Sometimes when I read my books, I say to myself, "This is good! Did I write that?" I enjoy double-purposing my books for reading and radio. Again, I have a deep appreciation for Steve Wick, who also produces "A Love Language Minute."

Both of my radio programs are aired on over four hundred stations.

> When I write scripts for my radio program, I enjoy revisiting my books, looking for ideas. Sometimes when I read my books, I say to myself, "This is good! Did I write that?"

One of the things I have learned from the radio ministry is the value of teamwork. This ministry would be impossible without Chris, Andrea, and Steve. They each have skills that I do not possess. When we pull those skills together and work as a team, we produce programs that are used of God to encourage listeners. The manner in which God brings a radio voice to an individual who is struggling, thus bringing help and hope, also amazes me. Through the years, many have shared stories of driving down the road and "accidentally" discovering one of our programs and hearing God speak to their specific need through something I said. That's when I know that the greatest member of our radio team is God. That is why we talk to Him before every recording session. We ask God to give us wisdom and then to match the message to the listener and accomplish His purposes.

When God's people team up with each other and with God, amazing things happen. I believe that is what the church is all about. The apostle Paul describes this reality in 1 Corinthians 12. We all have different spiritual gifts given to us by God. None of us can do everything, but when we each do our part, God's plans are accomplished. Let us never forget that every member of God's family has a role to play. Our greatest good is in being a part of His team.

The Speaking Ministry

People often ask if I enjoy writing. My honest answer is one with which many authors can agree. "I enjoy having written." The discipline of writing is not always enjoyable. It is the results of having written that keep me going. Knowing that books can go where I will never go and speak to people I will never see continues to motivate me.

However, when it comes to speaking, I truly enjoy it. I like the face-to-face encounter. I like to see the smiles or tears. I like to talk with people after I have spoken (or before). I enjoy interfacing with real people and hearing their journey.

When our children were young, I did not travel and speak. Of course, in those days, I'm not sure I had anything to say. I was still in the process of learning, growing, and listening. However, in the last thirty years, my speaking ministry has expanded. People have asked, "Do you enjoy traveling?" My response is, "I don't mind traveling. I am either reading or sleeping when I am on the plane, both of which I enjoy." Of course, there is the occasional "counseling session" when someone discovers that I am a counselor. Someone recently said, "You must see a lot of the country." I said, "I see whatever is between the airport and the venue where I am speaking." It is not the travel that excites me, it is the opportunity to share with people insights that I know will enrich their lives.

My speaking career, beyond my local community, began in the 1980s when I was invited to speak at the Billy Sunday Tabernacle in Winona Lake, Indiana. It was a week-long conference sponsored by Moody Bible Institute. I spoke at each of the morning sessions. At the end of the week, Jim Gwinn, assistant to Dr. George Sweeting, the president of Moody, asked if I would consider doing some conference speaking with Moody. I was shocked that he asked, but said I was open to the idea. The next few years, we did a number of FamilyLife conferences across the country. They were scheduled Sunday morning and evening through Wednesday night in five different churches in the city. We had five speakers who rotated through the churches. So each church heard each of the five speakers. The format was one that I had never seen before or since. Jim Gwinn planned and coordinated each of these events. One of the highlights for the speakers is that each day we had lunch together. That is where I got to know Mel Johnson (Tips for Teens radio), Greg Speck (youth specialist), Harold Sala (Guidelines for Living radio), and Steven Bly (a cowboy from Idaho, who authored numerous Western novels as well as books on family relationships). Recently, I talked with Jim Gwinn, and we had some good laughs remembering our conversations around the table.

In 1986, the centennial year of Moody Bible Institute, I was invited to join Jim, along with Dr. Kevin Leman, in speaking at several luncheons for pastors in various cities. The purpose was to celebrate what God had done over the past one hundred years and to seek to enrich and encourage the pastors in their own family relationships. Kevin and I had met earlier since he was sometimes on the team for the FamilyLife conferences discussed earlier. Kevin is a psychologist and has written numerous books on family relationships. He is also filled with humor. I will never forget one experience we had on this multi-city speaking tour.

We were in Florida, and Kevin had given an illustration of how parents teach children that there are consequences for their decisions. The illustration went something like this: Little Johnny comes to the dinner table, looks at the food, and says, "Ugh, I don't like it." Mom says, "That's fine, honey, you don't have to eat, you can run along and play." So Johnny runs off to play. One hour later, Johnny says, "Mom, I'm hungry." His mom says, "I bet you are, snookums. Could it have anything to do with the fact that you did not eat your dinner? You run along and play, and we will have breakfast in the morning." Kevin would say, "A child will not miss but one meal, and missing one meal will not hurt a child."

Well, when lunch was served to the pastors and to us, it was fish. Kevin did not like that particular kind of fish, so he did not eat lunch. That afternoon we were in the car headed to the next city where we would have another pastors' luncheon. Jim was driving. I was in the passenger seat, and Kevin was in the back seat. Around 3:00 p.m. Kevin said, "Jim, if you see a fast-food place, could we stop briefly? I'm feeling hungry." To which Jim responded, "I bet you are, snookums. Could it have anything to do with the fact that you did not eat your lunch?" Jim never stopped, and we all had dinner together that night. The moral of that story is that speakers need to be willing to live by the principles they teach. May God help all of us.

I want to offer a special thanks to Jim Gwinn for the role he played in my life personally and professionally. Following Jim, I continued doing conferences with Moody under the leadership of Jim Wick, Jim Jenks, Rick Pierce, Calvin Robinson, and Kevin Utecht. Each of these men played a significant role in my speaking ministry. God used them to open doors that I would never have entered otherwise.

When Karolyn and I returned home from the Moody Conference at Winona Lake, Indiana, Karolyn told me that one afternoon while we were there, she sat down alone in the Billy Sunday Tabernacle to spend some time reflecting with God. She said, "Sitting there with God, I had the distinct sense that God was going to use you in some special way with Moody Bible Institute." She said, "I had no idea in what way, but I knew in my heart that you would work with Moody." In retrospect, she was certainly right about that. My relationship with Moody Publishers, Moody Radio, and Moody Conference Ministry has played a major role in my life.

From my perspective, the most fruitful of my speaking opportunities are the Saturday Marriage Conferences that I do under the umbrella of Moody Publishers. Here I have the opportunity to share five different topics: "Solving Conflicts Without Arguing," "The 5 Love Languages," "Initiating Positive Change," "Making Sex a Mutual Joy," and "How to Share the Things That Bug You." In this context, I also share the good news about how God fits into the marriage equation. I speak at fifteen of these conferences each year, and every week we have people invite Christ into their lives. Nothing is more important than our relationship with God.

One experience that made an indelible mark on my heart was speaking at Angola Prison in Louisiana. All the men present were in prison for life. I told them that I was going to try to help them understand why they felt loved growing up—or why they did not feel loved. So I shared the love language concept in that context. At the Q & A and comment time, one young man stood up and said, "I want to thank you for coming because for the first time in my life, I finally understand that my mother loves me. As you gave those love languages, I knew that my love language is physical touch, but my mother never hugged me. The only hug I remember getting from her was the day I left for prison. But today I realize that she spoke acts of service. She was a single mom. She had two jobs. She kept food on the table, she washed my clothes, and ironed my shirts. She was loving me. I just didn't get it because she was not speaking my love language. Now I get it. Mama loves me. Mama loves me. Mama loves me."

> When I was speaking at Angola Prison in Louisiana, one young man stood up and said, "For the first time in my life, I finally understand that my mother loves me. I just didn't get it because she wasn't speaking my love language. Mama loves me. Mama loves me."

By this time, tears where streaming down his face. I must admit, tears were also in my eyes.

In my counseling with young adults who are estranged from their parents, I have often used this story to help them understand why they did not feel loved by their parents. Many times they can look back and realize that their parents did love them; they were just expressing their love in a different love language. Many of these young adults have been reconciled with their parents when they were willing to share with their parents the love language concept and how they had misunderstood their parent's expressions of love. So thanks to the Angola inmate who influenced me in this powerful way.

Another area of ministry that has deeply impacted me is the opportunity to speak on numerous military bases, both in the United States and other countries. It all began when I received an email from Chaplain Christopher Dickey, who was stationed in Afghanistan. He asked if I would consider going to Fort Bragg, located in Fayetteville, North Carolina, and speak to the spouses of the soldiers deployed in Afghanistan. He wanted me to share with them the message of the five love languages. He said that if I could do this, he would arrange for a satellite connection, so his soldiers could view it as well. This was before the days of Zoom, Skype, etc. I agreed, and in a few weeks, Karolyn and I drove to Fort Bragg. The auditorium seated 250, so I gave the presentation three times: Friday evening, Saturday morning, and afternoon with a full house at each session. In Afghanistan, the soldiers were in a large white tent attending the same session as their spouse.

At the end of the presentation, they arranged for each individual to go to another room where they could have a five-minute private conversation with their deployed spouse. Some of the wives were bringing babies who were born after deployment. So the soldiers were seeing their baby for the first time. Karolyn and I were in the hallway greeting them as they came out, often with tears. It was a very emotional experience, one I will never forget. After that event, I began to receive invitations to other military bases. Later, at the requests of several chaplains, I joined with Jocelyn Green, a military wife, and wrote *The 5 Love Languages: Military Edition* which focuses on how to speak the love languages when deployed. So thank you, Chaplain Dickey, for opening up my ministry to military couples, which I have enjoyed greatly.

In recent years I have had many opportunities to speak to business groups and other nonreligious conferences. Usually these groups want me to speak about the love languages, or *The 5 Languages of Appreciation in the Workplace*, which I wrote with Dr. Paul White. Many educational organizations want me to speak to parents on *The 5 Love Languages of Children* or *The 5 Love Languages of Teenagers*. Or to teachers on *Discovering the 5 Love Languages at School: Grades 1–6*, which I wrote with D. M. Freed, a school counselor. In secular settings, I always respect their request not to be "religious." Of course, if in the Q & A someone asks, "Where do you get the motivation to love?" I can tell where I get my motivation, which as I have noted earlier, is my relationship with Christ. I have found that in most nonreligious settings, the leaders expect you to be who you are. After all, they know I am a pastor when they invite me.

> **On speaking to diverse groups: I have found that in most nonreligious settings, the leaders expect you to be who you are.**

The Speaking Ministry:
Around the World

Speaking in other cultures is always the greatest challenge. First of all is the actual travel, which can be physically draining. Then there is the language and the cultural differences. I have always been fortunate in having good translators, some of whom will warn me about certain cultural nuances that I need to know. I am always deeply grateful for this.

Of course, I cannot share all of my experiences in other countries, but I will share one of my most meaningful. In 2017 I traveled to the country of Hungary. I had been there years earlier speaking at a missionary conference in Budapest. However, this time I was going at the invitation of my Hungarian publisher. I discovered they had published thirty-two of my books in Hungarian. I was humbled when on Sunday night, before we began our speaking tour on Monday, I had the opportunity to speak to one hundred pastors and wives at the First Baptist Church in Budapest, the oldest Baptist church in Hungary—140 years old, to be exact. After speaking, pastors from many different denominations gathered around me and prayed that God's hand would be upon our week of ministry.

Later that evening, Kornel Herjeczki, the president of Harmat Publishing Foundation, told me the story of First Baptist Church. His father was once the pastor of this church. The church was bombed in World War II. Later it was taken over by the Communists. His father was removed as pastor and was taken to the countryside where Kornel grew up. The Communists ruled the country for forty years. When Kornel was in college, he and two of his friends got permission—very unusual in those Communist years—to travel to Oxford for a conference for Christian medical students. There he met John Stott, the well-known British pastor and author, and became aware of InterVarsity Press, a publisher of Christian books. He and his friends purchased some of these books, and when back on campus, translated some of them into Hungarian and used them in student study groups.

Kornel became a medical doctor. However, when the Communists finally left the country, he and his friends established the Hungarian Fellowship of Evangelical Students (called ME-KDSZ). Later, with the help of a few Christian people mainly from England, they decided to start a Christian publishing company in Hungary, which they named Harmat (DEW).

In a few years, Kornel left his medical practice and became the president of the company. For the first few years, they published books mainly focused on helping Christian students. Most of these were books published by InterVarsity Press, which was (and is) the publishing arm of InterVarsity Christian Fellowship, an international ministry to students. However, a few years before I arrived, they published *The 5 Love Languages*, and it became their bestseller. They realized that the country was hungry for help on marriage and family relationships. So they began publishing my other books.

I was again deeply humbled to know that I now had the opportunity to speak in four major cities in Hungary. On Monday night, our time in Debrecen was incredible. The largest Reformed Church in Hungary is located here. It dates from the time of the Reformation. They also have a school from kindergarten through university as well as a seminary. The school is nearly five hundred years old. They gave us a tour of the library, which has 500,000 books. I signed six of my books and gave them to the library. So, they now have 500,006 books. That evening, I spoke to 1,200 people on the five love languages. They were a very responsive group. Eva, my translator, is from Debrecen and went to the same school.

I will never forget my visit to Debrecen. It reminded me of my debt to those Christians in whose train I follow.

Each morning I did interviews with reporters from newspapers, magazines, radio, and television. I was amazed at the interest in relationships and the impact *The 5 Love Languages* had made in the Hungarian culture. On Tuesday we left at 2:00 p.m., drove to the town of Pécs, and repeated our evening meeting with a thousand in attendance—again a very responsive audience.

The following morning I was given a tour of Budapest. We went to the castle district, Parliament, St. Stephens Church, and Independence Square. Here we saw the monument to the Russian liberation of Hungary from the Germans. (Of course, they stayed for forty years and controlled Hungary.) The monument sits right in front of the US Embassy. However, the most emotionally moving thing I saw were the shoes along the Danube, where Jews were shot and pushed into the river during the Second World War. These are real shoes that have been bronzed. The Jews were required to remove their shoes and jewelry before they were shot and pushed into the water. I wept at the cruelty of men and prayed that someday love would prevail in human relationships.

In the afternoon I did a book signing at a local secular bookstore. WOW! We had 250 people who waited in line. The bookstore manager told Kornel this was five times more than they ever had for a book signing. I must have signed more than five hundred books. One lady had a suitcase full of books to give to her friends. Two people told me that the five love languages had saved their marriage. At the end, my hand was tired, but my heart was full.

Our next meeting was in Szeged. We drove through beautiful farmland. The city is a university town. On the ride to Szeged, I talked with Kornel's daughter and her friend, both of whom are Christian counselors. They have started a Christian counseling center called Aurum and have been joined by others. I was encouraged to hear of their effort to serve people who are struggling. I prayed that God would continue to guide their efforts. That evening seven hundred attended our meeting—a capacity crowd. Again the audience was very warm and responsive. In each of these venues, the publishers sold books before and after the events. I was amazed at the eagerness of people to read books on relationships.

Our last event was in Budapest in an auditorium that seated two thousand. It was sold out a month before I arrived. Kornel asked if I would be willing to do an afternoon event as well. I agreed, and that also sold out, full capacity. Again, I was amazed at the hunger for practical help in building marriage and family relationships.

At the end of our week, Kornel said to me, "This is the greatest thing we have ever done for our country." Of course, only God knows the results of the thousands of books that were sold that week. But I do know that God uses books to touch hearts and change lives. Knowing the history of the publishing company, I was so grateful to be a part of helping expand their outreach.

One evening I had dinner at Kornel's home with his wife, Anna, and their two grown sons and younger daughter. Anna made delicious goulash. Now, you did not think that I could go to Hungary and not eat goulash, did you? Actually, I ate goulash almost every day, but Anna's was the best.

I could have shared the privilege of speaking in Mexico, Costa Rica, Honduras, Puerto Rico, Peru, Brazil, Turkey, China, Korea, Singapore, Canada, England, Scotland, Germany, France, Belgium, Holland, Switzerland, Italy, Ukraine, and Benin, West Africa. However, I think you can now understand why I chose to share my visit to Hungary. I was amazed to see what God can do with lives that are committed to Him. Kornel and those who joined him in the publishing ministry were a great encouragement to me.

On why I don't leave my church work and simply write and speak: "I believe that the church is God's main method of reaching the world for Christ. Secondly, I need a church home, a family with whom I can share life."

As noted earlier, my vocation has been both focused and flexible. Focused in that the theme has been serving Christ by serving people. Focused in that I have served as associate pastor on the same church staff for fifty years. That may be a record, especially for a Baptist church. However, it has been flexible in that it has involved working with different age groups: youth, college age, single adults, and married couples. Flexible, as it has involved different avenues of ministry: camp director, college professor, educational administrator, pastor, counselor, author, speaker, and radio host. I am blessed to have the best of both worlds: focus and flexibility. Thus, I am never bored. I look forward to each new day with a spirit of adventure, knowing that God will direct my steps.

People have sometimes asked: "Why don't you leave the church and simply write and speak since you have so many open doors to do both?" My response is: "Two reasons, first, I believe that the church is God's main method of reaching the world for Christ. Secondly, I need a church home, a family with whom I can share life." I am fully aware that I will some-day step off the church staff, but even so, I would like to work as a volunteer. Why would I leave my church family?

Another question I often hear is: "What would you like to do if you retired?" My response is: "I would like to do what I am doing." As long as God gives me health, I plan to keep walking through the doors that He opens. When He is through with me, then I am through. I have no plans other than His plans. I only pray that He will keep my heart and guide my steps to the finish line.

THINGS I'VE LEARNED IN MY VOCATIONAL CAREER

1. That our life plans are not always God's life plans.
2. That His plans will always be better and often bigger than we ever dreamed.
3. That truly loving others is the most Christlike thing we can do.
4. That a "listening ear" is the first step in helping people.
5. That situations that seem hopeless to us are never hopeless if we turn to God.
6. That God is able to do exceedingly, abundantly above all that we could ask or think.

Epilogue

Telling the story of my "life lessons" has been an enjoyable journey for me. Looking back over eighty-plus years of God's direction in my life, I am greatly humbled. How He could take even my failures and use them to teach me, prepare me, and use me to help countless others—all this reveals His great mercy and grace.

I am deeply grateful for all the individuals who have been His instruments in impacting how I became me. Sometimes it was a one-time conversation in which you encouraged me, corrected me, or informed me. With others I have spent a lifetime of rubbing shoulders, celebrating birthdays, weddings, and funerals. We have had numerous conversations in which we shared life together. That is why I consider you my friends. I know that if I needed you, you would be there as quickly as possible, and I would do the same for you. In this book, I have mentioned by name only a few of those individuals. There are countless others, some geographically close and others scattered around the world. For all of you, I am grateful.

Some of those who have impacted my life greatly are already in heaven. Among those is my sister, Sandra Benfield. She and I both were married in the summer of 1961. She and her husband, Reid, continued to live in the area where we grew up, and God gave them three lovely daughters: Traci, Jill, and Allison. When my dad died at the age of eighty-five, Mom was no longer able to manage her three-level house. So Sandra and Reid purchased a house beside them and Mom joyfully moved in. The plan was that Sandra and Reid would take care of my mother as she got older. However, in reality, my mother and Reid ended up taking care of Sandra, who died at the age of fifty-eight after an eight-year battle with cancer. Sandra was a model for me in two areas: how to invest one's life in helping others and how to face death with calm assurance, fully trusting God. My gratitude for her life will only be expressed fully when we meet again in the presence of Christ.

I look back on my life and marvel at the journey. To see how God brought all the experiences of life together to accomplish His purposes is indeed amazing. I am keenly aware that none of this would have happened without the loving hand of mercy and grace extended to me (and all who believe) by Christ our Savior and Lord. My favorite hymn expresses my heart of gratitude. I have requested that this hymn be sung at my funeral when I cross from time into eternity and discover a whole new chapter of His plans for me:

I stand amazed in the presence
Of Jesus the Nazarene,
And wonder how he could love me,
A sinner, condemned, unclean.

For me it was in the garden
He prayed, "Not my will, but thine;"
He had no tears for his own griefs,
But sweat drops of blood for mine.

He took my sins and my sorrows,
He made them his very own;
He bore the burden to Calv'ry,
And suffered and died alone.

When with the ransomed in glory
His face I at last shall see,
'Twill be my joy through the ages
To sing of his love for me.

How marvelous! How wonderful!
And my song shall ever be;
How marvelous! How wonderful!
Is my Savior's love for me!*

Of all the impacts on my life's journey, none is greater than the amazing love, mercy, and grace of God.

---

* See Charles H. Gabriel, "I Stand Amazed in the Presence," Hymnary.org, 1905, https://hymnary.org/text/i_stand_amazed_in_the_presence.

Books Written or Coauthored by Gary Chapman

FROM NORTHFIELD PUBLISHING AND MOODY PUBLISHERS

Love Language® Titles

The 5 Love Languages: The Secret to Love That Lasts

The 5 Love Languages for Men: Tools for Making a Good Relationship Great

The 5 Love Languages of Children: The Secret to Loving Children Effectively, Gary Chapman and Ross Campbell

The 5 Love Languages of Teenagers: The Secret to Loving Teens Effectively

The 5 Love Languages Singles Edition: The Secret That Will Revolutionize Your Relationships

The 5 Love Languages Military Edition: The Secret to Love That Lasts, Gary Chapman with Jocelyn Green

A Teen's Guide to the 5 Love Languages: How to Understand Yourself and Improve All Your Relationships, Gary Chapman with Paige Hayley Drygas

Discovering the 5 Love Languages at School (Grades 1–6): Lessons That Promote Academic Excellence and Connections for Life, Gary Chapman and D. M. Freed

God Speaks Your Love Language: How to Experience and Express God's Love

Seen. Known. Loved. 5 Truths About God and Your Love Language, Gary Chapman and R. York Moore

The Love Languages Devotional Bible: Spend Each Day Growing in the Word of God and Drawing Closer as a Couple (NLT version)

What Are the 5 Love Languages?: The Official Book Summary

A Perfect Pet for Peyton, Gary Chapman and Rick Osborne

Penny's Perfect Present, Gary Chapman and Rick Osborne

A Marriage Carol, Gary Chapman and Chris Fabry

Workplace Titles

The 5 Languages of Appreciation in the Workplace: Empowering Organizations by Encouraging People, Gary Chapman and Paul White

Rising Above a Toxic Workplace: Taking Care of Yourself in an Unhealthy Environment, Gary Chapman, Paul White, and Harold Myra

Sync or Swim: A Fable About Workplace Communication and Coming Together in a Crisis, Gary Chapman, Paul White, and Harold Myra

101 Conversation Starters Series

101 Conversation Starters for Couples, Gary Chapman and Ramon Presson

101 More Conversation Starters for Couples, Gary Chapman and Ramon Presson

101 Conversation Starters for Families, Gary Chapman and Ramon Presson

Love + Hope Series

Holding On to Love After You've Lost a Baby: The 5 Love Languages for Grieving Parents, Gary Chapman and Candy McVicar

Building Love Together in Blended Families: The 5 Love Languages and Becoming Stepfamily Smart, Gary Chapman and Ron R. Deal

Sharing Love Abundantly in Special Needs Families: The 5 Love Languages for Parents Raising Children with Disabilities, Gary Chapman and Jolene Philo

Keeping Love Alive as Memories Fade: The 5 Love Languages and the Alzheimer's Journey, Gary Chapman, Edward Shaw, and Deborah Barr

General Titles

5 Simple Ways to Strengthen Your Marriage . . . When You're Stuck at Home Together

A Couple's Guide to a Growing Marriage: A Bible Study

Anger: Taming a Powerful Emotion

Choose Greatness: 11 Wise Decisions That Brave Young Men Make, Gary Chapman and Clarence Shuler

Extraordinary Grace: How the Unlikely Lineage of Jesus Reveals God's Amazing Love, Gary Chapman and Chris Fabry

How to Really Love Your Adult Child: Building a Healthy Relationship in a Changing World, Gary Chapman and Ross Campbell

Loving Your Spouse When You Feel Like Walking Away: Real Help for Desperate Hearts in Difficult Marriages

Married and Still Loving It: The Joys and Challenges of the Second Half, Gary Chapman and Harold Myra

One More Try: What to Do When Your Marriage Is Falling Apart

Screen Kids: 5 Skills Every Child Needs in a Tech-Driven World, Gary Chapman and Arlene Pellicane

Grandparenting Screen Kids: How to Help, What to Say, and Where to Begin, Gary Chapman and Arlene Pellicane

The DIY Guide to Building a Family That Lasts: 12 Tools for Improving Your Home Life, Gary Chapman and Shannon Warden

The Family You've Always Wanted: Five Ways You Can Make It Happen

The Marriage You've Always Wanted

The Marriage You've Always Wanted Event Experience

The Marriage You've Always Wanted Small Group Experience

Things I Wish I'd Known Before My Child Became a Teenager

Things I Wish I'd Known Before We Got Married

Things I Wish I'd Known Before We Became Parents, Gary Chapman with Shannon Warden

When Sorry Isn't Enough: Making Things Right with Those You Love, Gary Chapman and Jennifer Thomas

Falling for You Again, Gary Chapman and Catherine Palmer

Happily Ever After: Six Secrets to a Successful Marriage

It Happens Every Spring, Gary Chapman and Catherine Palmer

Life Promises for Couples

Love as a Way of Life: Seven Keys to Transforming Every Aspect of Your Life

The Love as a Way of Life Devotional: A Ninety-Day Adventure That Makes Love a Daily Habit, Gary Chapman and Elisa Stanford

Love Is a Verb: Stories of What Happens When Love Comes Alive

Love Language Minute for Couples: 100 Days to a Closer Relationship

Love Notes for Couples

Now You're Speaking My Language: Honest Communication & Deeper Intimacy for a Stronger Marriage

Summer Breeze, Gary Chapman and Catherine Palmer

The Four Seasons of Marriage: Secrets to a Lasting Marriage

The One Year Love Language Minute Devotional

Winter Turns to Spring, Gary Chapman and Catherine Palmer

Acknowledgments

Earlier, I noted the significance of the Chapman Team at Moody Publishers in all of my publications. The present team is composed of John Hinkley, Janis Todd, Betsey Newenhuyse, Zack Williamson, Randall Payleitner, Richard Knox, Ashley Torres, and Joel Stombres. Again in this book, I want to express my deepest gratitude for each of them. As always, they have made it happen.

I also want to thank other members of the Chapman Team through the years: Greg Thornton, Ed Santiago, Judy Tollberg, Steve Gemeiner, Grace Park, Jim Jenks, John Trent, and Becky Byrd. I view all of you as extended family, along with the rest of the Moody Publishers staff. God has used each of you in a significant way in my life's journey.

I want to express my appreciation to my coauthors whom I noted earlier but did not name: Arlene Pellicane, Ross Campbell, Catherine Palmer, Ed Shaw, Debbie Barr, Jolene Philo, Paul White, Jocelyn Green, Chris Fabry, Harold Myra, Shannon Warden, Clarence Shuler, Candy McVicar, Ron Deal, and York Moore. Each of you have played a significant role in my life and ministry, for which I am deeply grateful.

In my daily role as a writer, pastor, counselor, and speaker, four ladies have played a significant role: Anita Hall, Tricia Kube, and Debbie Barr have been my administrative assistants over the years. They have processed the many phone calls, emails, and text messages from those inquiring about counseling, speaking, or interviews. I can never fully express my deep appreciation for their impact on my life. The fourth lady (in case you are wondering) is my wife, Karolyn. As noted earlier, she edits all of my books, and this one is no exception. Two are definitely better than one.